surviving the unexpected
WILDERNESS EMERGENCY

Written by GENE FEAR

Experienced outdoorsman
Mountaineer
Volunteer Rescue Team Member
Survival Instructor
Author of
OUTDOOR LIVING - MRA
Co-author of
SURVIVING the UNEXPECTED
Author of numerous outdoor articles
and safety publications

Standard Book Number 0-913724-02-5
Library of Congress Card Number 73-78035
Printed in the United States of America

Copyright © 1972
Revised Edition
Copyright — 1975 by Eugene H. Fear
Artwork — Richard Pargeter

SURVIVAL KNOWLEDGE

Published by
SURVIVAL EDUCATION ASSOCIATION
9035 Golden Given Rd.
Tacoma, Washington 98445

The author is an experienced outdoorsman who has encountered more than his fair share of outdoor emergencies. Foreign travel, back country living, farming, flying, business, and family furnished good beginning information. His volunteer service to improve outdoor safety in recreation for 20 years proved a different approach to recreation safety was needed. Less emphasis on safety techniques and more education on why and how environmental stress effects the total body while away from modern technology.

During six years as chairman of the national safety education effort of Mountain Rescue Association, he introduced thousands of teachers, leaders, and interested individuals to his concept of survival. Eight years of teaching survival proved a valuable asset in determining what was needed.

Credit is due many friends and fellow volunteer rescue teammates, doctors, and research publication authors for the information necessary for this complex study on human body survival anywhere.

TABLE OF CONTENTS

SELF-RELIANCE IS SURVIVAL

Any emergency that threatens life will not be pleasant. Few of us relish the thought of having to face such discomforts as hunger, thirst, cold, heat, or fearfulness. Modern technology and government-provided security have accustomed us to so many conveniences that many of us could not cope with daily problems such as those faced by our forefathers, the pioneers. All too few moderns are self-reliant, self-disciplined, or have the self-confidence to fend and provide for themselves from raw nature.

Being self-sufficient amid modern technology is not the same as being self-sufficient in a natural or man-made disaster, or alone in a stormy wilderness. In one you have instant relief for nearly all of your needs and desires. In the other you are dependent only upon yourself and your ability to be self-sufficient to survive long enough to get out of your predicament; to survive long enough for someone to bring you the necessities of life, or for you to acquire air, shelter, water, warmth, and energy.

In your unexpected survival experience you will have to accept the situation with just what you have at the moment it happens, where it happens, and how it happens. Your problem-solving must be based on the known body enemies that threaten life, their priority of influence, and their severity of threat to your life. Acting out the solution will depend upon your body's energy supply, the environmental factors involved, your ability or non-ability to recognize the danger, your skills and abilities, and the knowledge to improvise the defenses needed.

The purpose of this book is to put forth education about human limitations in natural environments so that those leaving civilization may be better able to maintain well-being and cope with unexpected situations. Each person has his own level of competence and comfort zone; both will be challenged by the fury of natural storms or disaster.

NATURE'S PRIORITY: **Take care of the brain first.**
Then it will take care of you.

The gravest problem of all will be mental. Combating the fear of your own weakness, fear of the unknown, and fear of discomfort. Survival is nearly 100 percent a mental challenge, with all decisions of life resting upon your knowledge of what the body needs and how to acquire those needs.

Even in a survival emergency you cannot be running and working all the time. Your body needs rest just as badly as it needs air, shelter and water. Regardless of the impending dangerous future or the terrifying past experience, a moment of rest is necessary to refuel the muscles. Use this moment to refresh the brain. Yes, even the mind needs rest from the frustration and anxiety of the emergency. One way to combat mental stress during body rest is to *enjoy the moment.* Stop. Look and comprehend what is about you at that *moment,* wherever it is. That *moment* is yours and there will never be another exactly like it. The clouds, scenery, wildlife, sunlight are yours alone. Enjoy it. That *moment,* with all of its wonderment, can instill a calm perspective that rests your mind and eases the fear and anxiety.

Regardless of the anticipated dangers and past frustrations, there is some wonder and beauty in everything about you. *If you allow yourself to see them.* You know it is there — look for it. Once you see it, a wonderful feeling engulfs you. The fear and frustration leaves for a moment. Your tired body relaxes and you spend a *moment* amid splendor you will never enjoy again.

Many great explorers, scientists, and philosophers practiced this technique of resting the brain. It works equally well in the troubled times of survival. Enjoy mentally that *moment* of body rest. There is beauty in the fury of a storm, and some enjoyment in nearly every happening. When you look at the brighter side of today, this hour, *this moment,* your mind and body are calmed.   Your brain is your best survival tool.

Unknown factors in any unexpected emergency are numerous and variable. Some compound others. Some counteract others. Some affect the priorities of life. Others influence the mind, causing panic or loss of body control. Since keeping the body alive is the problem that must be solved, knowledge about the priorities of life and the body's common enemies would help determine the best course of action in sustaining life during the emergency. This knowledge must be within your brain before you can recognize and solve the problems that can threaten life.

1 ⊙ ⊙ ANTICIPATING A PROBLEM

TRAVEL AWAY FROM CIVILIZATION

The intent of this book is to help man in his transition from city living to outdoor living by making the reader aware of some of the problems he is likely to encounter.

Because of the variety of outdoor activities, the changeable elements, and varied environments, the text problems and their recommended actions have been generalized. Outdoor travel as this book refers to it is done by every person every day. Outdoors will be thought of as being away from shelter and warmth, where a person is exposed to nature's elements such as wind, rain, and cold. Outdoor travel has no boundaries; it is used by persons around the home, farm, beach or mountain. It is not something new or different; and everyone has, at some time or other, experienced the consequences of disregarding the following common sense practices of outdoor travel.

There is no substitute for experience in all outdoor recreation activities, but the knowledge to be able to recognize potential dangers would be beneficial in every activity away from civilization, where most dangers are expected to have warning signs, flags or yellow lights. The modern city dweller often forgets that natural wilderness dangers do not display these warnings, or the fact that he will not have immediate aids such as telephones, supplies, ambulances, direction signs, or warmth and shelter.

The pioneers, whom we attempt to emulate in our outdoor adventures, lived in an era when their daily existence necessitated coping with natural hazards to their survival. Then all travel was regulated by the weather and the terrain, not a time schedule.

4

"Careless Ev"

SHORT FOR CARELESS EVERYBODY

Modern technology has released today's man from many of the daily responsibilities that the pioneer shouldered, especially in the areas of warmth, shelter, judgment and safety. Modern man has altogether too much faith and reliance in push-buttons, dials and signals to combat the forces of nature. He has relinquished much of his self-government and safety responsibility to political agencies. In the cities and other areas of overpopulation, this has become necessary. But when modern man undertakes an outdoor activity which takes him away from these modern conveniences, he often finds he is unable to cope with the multitude of decisions necessary to sustain life and safe travel.

Choosing your companions for an outing is extremely important. Their physical strength and mental attitude can affect the enjoyment; their outdoor abilities or limitations and the equipment they carry or do not carry will contribute to the success or failure of your outing.

Be sure you are familiar with all the potential dangers along your route and consider any delays or problems you may encounter. Allow ample time for an unhurried trip. Study good topographical maps and inquire about trails, campsites, roads, etc., from recent visitors to the area; or ask the local land management officials, such as Rangers, Game Department, and Forest Service personnel.

Outdoor recreationists should consider the present weather and the future weather before and during any outing. If weather is threatening, plan the outing for another weekend — or plan and prepare for the worst it may offer. Weather contributes in some way to nearly all accidental survival emergencies.

Weather not only adds to the complexity of the trip, it affects the morale of the party; most wet, cold hikers get careless. Fog obscures the landmarks and makes outdoor navigation difficult, if not impossible. Rain or snow makes any outdoor travel hazardous, especially in descending on rocks or heather. Trails become muddy and slippery; streams may wash out the crossings; and thunder and lightning always warrant a hasty retreat from high points.

Wind is your greatest enemy because it can quickly steal your limited supply of energy through loss of body heat. Unless your party has planned and prepared for threatening weather, it is wise to retreat whenever adverse weather strikes your outing.

Almost everyone has, at some time, experienced discomfort because he had not planned properly for the activity in which he was engaged. Small discomforts do not often endanger life, but they have a way of taking away all of the enjoyment of the outing.

In our modern society many of us live and work within limited budgets and preset hours for relaxation. Such regulation limits the length and breadth of our enjoyment of outdoor activities, so we tend to work hard and travel fast to wring the maximum enjoyment out of every minute of our leisure time.

Think back — how many minor discomforts put a blight on your enjoyment of an outing?

Wet clothes — because you didn't prepare for rain.
A blister — because of the wrong shoes.
Insects — and you had no repellent.
Fatigued or bone tired — because of too long a trip.
The cold wind on a shady trail when you were wearing shorts.

Even in the city we have discomforts because we venture out without forethought. Have you ever hid behind a lamp post or tree to get some shelter from wind or rain?

Not all outings that are completed without mishap are conducted in a safe manner. Some people are lucky; some days are always sunny, and some storms are quickly over.

After the planning and preparation are completed you should consider the fact that a possible accident could happen that would delay your party for hours or even days. Have you mentally prepared the loved ones at home for a possible delay? Have you written down your travel area, route you will use, names of companions and the model of car, its color, and the license of the car you plan to use to get to your outdoor travel area? It is wise to list even the equipment you carry and physical limitations of members of the party, along with the approximate time you plan to return and any probable delays you think you may encounter.

This written note should be left with a responsible person and made available to Search and Rescue officials should you not return as scheduled. It will be a vital message that will allow search groups to move properly and quickly to aid you should you need them. Also, sign out with authorities (rangers, Forest Service) if possible.

Signing out and back in through the available Forest Service and National Park registration system is for your own benefit. It will in no way restrict or inhibit your freedom, but rather is designed to be a useful tool to help you, should you encounter difficulty. However, you should be sure to advise the responsible person in town should you change your plans and go to a different area. Search officials may look for you only in the area you stated you would be visiting.

All wilderness travel should have a minimum of four persons in the party. In an emergency two go for help and one stays with the victim.

Distance travelled in the wilderness is measured in hours. All persons should have a knowledge of first aid. In a medical emergency help will be many hours or days away, depending upon the area.

Survival will demand being self-sufficient when away from civilization.

PLANNING OUTDOOR TRAVEL

Planning Your Day: Think about your future needs.

What does your activity demand? Each activity requires different planning — different clothing, different equipment, different amounts of energy, for differences in weather and environment.

Protective Measures to Consider for Non-exercise Activities:

Layer system of clothing. Several layers of loose-fitting clothing that have airsacs in the weave. Wool for warmth. Proper foot and ankle protection. Easy-on-easy-off type clothing to allow body temperature regulation.

Anticipation of wind chill heat loss, conduction heat loss.

Adequate body shelter from rain, wind, cold, sun.

Adequate energy and water restoration.

Adequate skin and eye protection from sun's rays.

Points to Consider in Planning Physical Exercise:

Avoid overheating by removing a layer of clothing; provide ventilation by opening.

Avoid restriction of circulation by tight clothing.

Perspiration — wet underclothes are hard to dry; ventilate.

Pace affects heart and lungs — slow down. Consider fatigue and its effect.

When away from civilization and the immediate supply of warmth, shelter and energy, you alone are responsible to maintain a reserve of energy — energy that cannot be stored like canned foods for immediate use. It must be replenished from high energy foods eaten in small amounts but often during the trip.

Body heat is energy, and loss of body heat thru chilling uses your reserve energy. Fast pace, sweating, running, worry, and panic all use enormous amounts of body energy. Excessive use of your energy supply will cause exhaustion.

Recommendations for Controlling Body Energy and Heat Loss During Exercise:

Layer System of Clothing. Activity dictates type and style of clothing worn: loose fitting, easy-on-easy-off clothing to provide ventilation and lessen restriction on muscles used.

Swimming	Few types of clothing are interchangeable. Otherwise
Skiing	we would swim with clothes on and hike barefooted.
Skin diving	Choose proper clothing.
Hiking	

Pace. Heart, lungs and muscles determine speed of travel. Body condition has little bearing on distance traveled, only on the *time* needed to travel the distance. Never exercise strenuously on a full stomach. Slow the pace during warm-up period before strenuous action.

Perspiration. Body heat loss and water loss — both must be replaced. Ration your sweat, not your water. Excessive perspiration causes salt deficiency that can cause cramps or fatigue as well as dehydration. In cold conditions, perspiration wetness on underclothes causes excessive chilling when activity stops. Body heat loss is speeded by conduction where wet clothing touches skin. Ventilate — remove a layer of clothing — or slow down.

Rest

Short rest stops can partially remove the detrimental waste products of muscle movement and allow the circulation system to refuel the muscles.

Sleep

Inadequate sleep prior to a strenuous day of muscle activity will affect energy/fatigue factors of the day. Inadequate sleep after strenuous activity does not allow removal of all the detrimental waste products from the activity. You must have sleep so that the body's automatic processes can repair and regain its chemical balance.

Continued shortages of sleep will affect judgment, reasoning, reflexes, muscle coordination; and if prolonged will effect a fatigue debt that can cause collapse from exhaustion.

Fatigue:

Fatigue will lessen your enjoyment and increase the accident potential of your activity.

Uphill: Take slower steps and short rest stops. If windy provide cover; wind chill can cause fatigue and energy loss. Nibble energy foods.

Downhill: Most accidents happen on descent because of fatigue from going up. Visibility is often restricted and footing insecure. Use caution and slow down.

SLOW DOWN YOUR PACE
or SUFFER THE MISERY OF FATIGUE

Exhaustion:

You are tired, so you sit or lie down to rest. Clothing may be wet from perspiration, allowing wind chill to quickly lower the body temperature below the normal, and then accidental hypothermia gains a foothold and you can deplete your remaining energy very quickly.

Other Planning Considerations:

In outdoor travel, consideration must be given to other facets of the activity which have a decided effect upon the success of the venture:

Effect of Weather Elements on your Activity.

Visibility	Wetness	Frostbite
Cold	Heat	Blindness
Wind chill	Dryness	

Each area will be different and the weather elements will vary. Prepare for the activity and its needed equipment. Plan for the activity with weather forecasts or from informed sources. Carry or have immediately available the necessary equipment for anticipated weather, and have immediately available the necessary body and skin protection. Many outdoor trips are cancelled or turn back because of lack of foresight in choosing equipment and clothing to meet the challenge of deteriorating weather. Clothing is easy to take off — but cannot be put on if it is at home or left at the car.

Potential Dangers of your Activity. Analyze equipment needed for body protection and for safe participation in your sport. Know the characteristics and dangers of tools (axes, knives, skis, boats, stoves, fuels) and be familiar with their proper use. Environmental dangers may include avalanches (snow, land, mud), water hazards, mechanical dangers, falling. The responsibility for safe outdoor travel is yours alone.

Extra protection for head, legs, feet.

Clothing adequate for rain, cold and wind.

Consider the safety equipment needs appropriate to the activity.

Environmental Dangers.

Avalanches (snow, mud, rocks) — recognize them and detour.

Water (boats, flotation, waves) — know the limitations of the equipment being used.

Mountains (cliffs, glaciers, loose rock) — travel only with an experienced leader who has technical knowledge of the hazards. If you are alone in mountainous terrain, slow down, pick the safest route, or detour around danger areas.

Terrain (cliffs, beaches, rocks, swamps, water) — each must be evaluated before leaving home or inquired about before traveling on. Use caution; anticipate and analyze the danger.

Mechanical dangers (cars, boats, planes, scooters, skateboards, surfboards, skis) — all have inherent motion hazards that must be respected and understood, as well as operational rules and limitations that require attention of the user. Safe operation or adjustment of safety equipment rests with the user.

Velocity dangers — A falling rock can be fatal. Velocity plays a damaging role when the skier meets a tree or a hiker slips on a precipitous switchback trail.

Thoughtful planning and prudent choice of safety equipment for your activity is necessary to help prevent injury. There are many safety aids to minimize injury; understand their use and mechanics thoroughly. The responsibility for maintenance and adjustment is yours alone.

Food Intake is Needed for Restoration of Energy Used:

Immediate availability of food — if not readily available, carry it.

Type of energy foods needed and amount should be compatible with length of trip. Strenuous activity demands more carbohydrates.

All Activities demand water. Carry water with you in all unfamiliar areas.

In all outdoor travel, planning is necessary. Choosing companions of comparable physical ability will make the trip smoother. Choose the proper equipment for the area. Pace the activity to allow an energy reserve. Turn back when adverse conditions set in. Evaluate all potential danger areas before proceeding. Most important — leave information as to your area of travel, transportation, companions, and approximate return time.

*The less experienced the
Hiking Group —
The more experienced the
Leader should be.*

Place of Activity:

Distance involved	By car, on foot or swimming — each requires quite different planning. Distance should be measured in hours required to receive assistance, if needed.
Time involved	Daylight or darkness — turn back with ample time to reach car or camp.
Weather expected	Always plan for the worst Mother Nature can unleash upon you.
Alternate plans	You may have to go to the beach instead of the mountains (or vice versa because they are crowded, closed or contaminated). Be prepared to change plans.

Responsibilities of the Activity:

To private property
Get permission to treaspass.
To others in the party
Courtesy and consideration; keeping together.
To the leader
Keep him aware of your whereabouts and approximate return time.
To parents
Knowledge of whereabouts and approximate return time.
To authorities
Sign out or permission.
To self
If what you do causes delays, injuries or damage, you, yourself, carry the responsibility of the action.

2 ∘∘   PROBLEM ANALYSIS

THE CHALLENGE TO STAY ALIVE
All Alone - Under Adverse Wilderness Conditions

In this modern age each of us must survive everyday. We eat, drink, sleep, shelter our bodies, and use our muscles to move about and operate a multitude of mechanical devices everyday. As long as we remain in a familiar environment, the lack or failure of any of these accustomed benefits will normally pose only an inconvenience.

Some of these same everyday occurences may become a matter of life or death in an unfamiliar or hostile environment.

In the familiar city, shelter is rarely given a thought. If we are cold we turn up the thermostat. If it is stormy we reach for a coat or run from house to car. Rarely do we experience the sting of wind chill or the pain of bone cold hands and feet. We don't give a second thought to the human body's regulatory processes that are needed to maintain its delicate heat balance. Regulatory processes of heat production represent a primary burden on the body, and any change sets up consequential disturbances which increase the total burden.

Outdoor survival is maintaining this delicate heat balance and conserving enough energy to continue to produce the heat to maintain this optimum temperature. Your greatest enemy, as you stand alone against hostile weather elements, will be anything that takes away or adds to this temperature. A few degrees either way in body temperature and you become incapable of thinking or acting rationally.

Adapting to the situation and its environment requires the ability, versatility and resourcefulness to provide the adequate body shelter necessary and to acquire the liquids necessary to prevent dehydration. All else, save injury or bleeding, is of secondary importance in delaying the hour of death and being alive when rescued.

In any unexpected survival experience you will have to accept the situation with just what you have at the moment it happens, where it happens, and how it happens. Your problem-solving must be based on the known body enemies that threaten life, their priority of influence, and their severity of threat to your life. Acting out the solution will depend upon your body's energy supply, the environmental factors involved, your ability or non-ability to recognize the danger, your skills and abilities, and the knowledge to improvise the defenses needed.

Unknown factors in any unexpected emergency are too numerous and so variable that they cannot be listed. Some compound others. Some counteract others. Some affect the priorities of life. Others influence the mind, causing panic or loss of body control.

Since keeping the body alive is the problem that must be solved, knowledge about the priorities of life and the body's common enemies would help determine the best course of action in sustaining life during the emergency.

Using Your Brain to Conserve Your Body's Energy under Adverse Conditions

Talk about survival must be hypothetical because each situation will be different, and every person will react differently. You will be forced to live one hour at a time, trying to stay alive.

Survival crisis in our modern age will generally be short term. Search may begin soon after you are missed, but searches take time. Your greatest concern is conserving what energy you have, improving your situation, returning to civilization if you can, or sitting and awaiting the searchers and aiding them with signals, if possible.

Few places are left in America more than one day's travel on foot from civilization of some kind. If you tell someone where you are going and when you'll be back, you will be missed and reported as such to the local sheriff or National Park. A search may be initiated after allowing time for normal travel delays.

Survival of the strongest is not always true. More likely it is the survival of the "thinkingest," *for your brain is your best survival tool.* That the thinking man survives is a proven theory, because it is you against the elements, outwitting them, choosing the best route over unfamiliar terrain, and self-management to conserve the body's energy. Panic becomes your enemy, necessitating positive control over physical and mental activities to assure conservation of energy, recognizing natural resources, natural shelters, and sources of warmth and energy. The thinking man will have ready resources with him — he will carry emergency food, warmth, and shelter on wilderness travels or hazardous journeys.

In any survival situation you are suddenly forced to rely upon your own resources with no immediate help to turn to. Your present physical energy must be conserved and the urge to panic (run for home) must be subdued. The situation must be analyzed for dangers, ready resources, possible natural resources and future problems to expect.

Possible Problems to Think About and Recommendations of Action to Take

Analysis of your present *daylight* situation:

Location   Improve it if dangerous. Move, if necessary, to warmer, more protected area. In desert sun find shade; do not travel.

Weather   Find warmth and insulation or shade. Find shelter from rain, snow, wind, to preserve body heat. Shade to prevent heat gain.

Darkness	Prepare for it in daylight. Find water and shelter and make camp early. Gather fuel for warmth. Use this forced inactivity time to think out your problems and plan for tomorrow.
Restricted Visibility	Sit it out or plan to use artificial aids (map, compass, flashlight).
Signals	Aid searchers with all available signals. Fire signals at night, smoke signals, panels, code, flags and blazes in daylight. Audible signals. Any sound that is unusual or contrasts with the environmental sounds.
Physical dangers	Take corrective steps. Protect from falling, drowning, further injury to self; protect from insects or any other apparent hazards.

Analysis of how *darkness* will affect your situation:

Lack of visibility	Generally restricts safe travel, as there are too many possibilities for injury. Restricts shelter building and fuel gathering.
Increased cold	Prepare in advance. Burrow in. Confine the space you must heat.
On snow	It is colder. Find insulation.
On Desert	Travel at night when it is cooler, if it is light enough to see; camp during the heat of the day.
Dangers	Injury due to falling, loss of direction.

Analysis of your situation should include travel to civilization, especially in a long-term survival situation, with no hope of searchers or being missed by someone. If supplies are limited, ration food, water and fuel, and conserve energy. Travel only in daylight, near water and clearings. Recognize physical limitations.

To stay alive over extended time periods requires rigid control over mental and physical activity to conserve maximum energy.

In any survival situation these are the first problems to analyze and their recommended action.

SPRINGTIME'S THUNDER

Danger to self
If injured, stop bleeding; administer first aid. Protect from weather — provide shelter, clothing to stop body heat loss to air and ground.

Danger to location
From side / From above / From below
Vehicles, avalanches, fire, building collapse, floods, explosion, more collisions, animals, lightning, storms. Move to a safer location as soon as practical.

Danger from the elements
Rain ⎫
Wind ⎬ Seek any shelter, ready made, natural,
Snow ⎪ or improvised.
Sun ⎭

Lightning
Squat down away from metal, trees, caves, peaks.

Fire ⎫ Improve your
Floods ⎬ situation in any
Earthquakes ⎭ way possible.

Have you ever watched animals when a storm breaks? They head for the timber and their burrows. It is not because they are afraid of the storm, but they are instinctively avoiding wind chill. People, too, should find shelter. This is the only protection available unless you are carrying it.

Conservation of Body Heat

When exposed to weather, some type of body protection is helpful — and may be absolutely necessary to sustain life.

Rain	Wets clothing, causing rapid cooling through evaporation and conduction of body heat. Dry clothing loses 90% of its insulation value when it gets wet.
	Put on rain clothing, find shelter (cave, under tree, logs).
Wind	Causes body heat loss through convection. Increases moisture evaporation. Wind can blow away body heat faster than you can produce it.
	Put on wind resistant clothing; find lee side shelter or any kind.
Cold Air (still)	Causes body heat loss through radiation of body heat into colder air.
	Insulate with clothing, or snow shelter or confined area. Add warmth from fire or sunshine.
Water	Body heat loss through very rapid cooling of the skin by conduction (contact with colder water).
	Dry off immediately. Remove wet clothing and wind dry, fire dry or freeze dry and beat out ice crystals. Initiate some alternate heat source — fire, body-to-body, sun's rays — to restore lost body heat.
Sun	Loss of energy due to heat gain or dehydration from sweating.

Seek shade. Cover exposed portions of body. Avoid over-exertion. In desert dig into the cool earth, improvise shade. Do not travel. Maintain adequate salt intake. Don't try to preserve your water supply — drink it as needed.

Reflect sun.

Cover face, body, and eyes if on snow or water.

You Must Have Water to Live

A source of water is an absolute necessity. Obtaining pure water can be a problem in certain areas. Boil all water before drinking, when in doubt. Running mountain waters are fairly safe to drink in small amounts. Always carry more than necessary. To avoid fatal dehydration it may be necessary to drink dirty water (unboiled or unpurified) rather than go without.

Food is of Minor Importance for Short-term Survival

Wasting energy searching for berries or edible plants is not advised. The energy gained is often not worth the energy expended, unless they are readily available. Food is a great pacifier but not essential to short-term survival.

If You Have Not Left a Trip Schedule

If you are positive no one will miss you and report you lost or missing, and no search may be expected, attempt to travel to civilization. You should have approximately ten days' body energy if you conserve it. Travel slowly and only when you can see. Protect the body from heat loss and dehydration. Travel downhill, by the easiest route, or follow a straight line. Stay near water but avoid swamps, brush and blowdowns.

YOUR SURVIVAL WILL BE YOUR PROBLEM TO SOLVE

The rescuers' problem is to carry you back — When you cannot solve the problem of staying alive long enough to —

Get out of your predicament;
Acquire the necessities of life (air, shelter, water, warmth, food);
Allow others to bring the necessities of life to you.

Since you alone are master of your destiny — anywhere, any time — keeping the body alive and functioning must be the first and chief concern whenever away from civilization or modern technology.

Your body has certain priorities in its requirements to sustain life. You alone can determine the value, or order of importance.

Your body requires basic necessities. Only you can analyze what is necessary immediately.

The threat to life during any unexpected emergency will be centered around certain body enemies that attack the body in a variety of ways. Sometimes singly, sometimes in concert — but always these enemies will possess a threat to the process of sustaining life without assistance or guidance from others. You must know how these can harm you and how to prevent them from getting too great a hold upon the body.

For you to solve the problem of staying alive —
You must recognize a challenge or a threat against your life.
You must react to the body's problem indicators.
You must ascertain the priorities needed to maintain life.
You must combat the body's enemies that threaten life.

These demands must be met regardless of the cost in material things or energy expenditure.

It's your body — and your problem.

3 ∘ ∘   PROBLEM INDICATORS

YOUR BODY'S PHYSIOLOGICAL PROBLEM INDICATORS

These problem indicators can be man's greatest allies in a survival situation. Each indicator tells a story of what is happening within the body. Each has its own critical implications — each is a danger sign. Each has a cause, which the alert outdoorsman should recognize and correct, or at least minimize.

To live in harmony with the outdoor environment, man must be aware of the psychological and physiological reactions that may develop within his body because of hostile weather conditions. The length of time a person is exposed and the severity of the weather can be the most important factors to consider in determining the thermal and physical state of his body.

The effects of exposure to heat or cold are so unpredictable that they often sneak up on the unwary outdoorsman, sapping his energy reserves slowly but persistently. This can turn a pleasant outing into a misadventure that could have been avoided had he recognized and heeded nature's warnings. Nearly everyone begins his outdoor activity anticipating enjoyment, relaxation, and some self-fulfillment. In fact, during planning and the fore-part of the outing, this is the driving force that makes the trip possible. Fortunately, the majority of our adventures are enjoyable and end with a feeling of accomplishment and gentle tiredness that is remembered only as the cost of a pleasant day.

Occasionally a trip will start as an enjoyable outing, but slowly deteriorate to something less desirable, if not outright unpleasant. This could be caused by weather, emotions, or such a little thing as a blister on the foot, clothing getting damp, or a sardine can in the pack that pokes the ribs. Whatever the reason for the discomfort, if not corrected it will become miserable, then eventually unbearable. When the outing becomes miserable it is likely the traveler will abort the trip and hurry back to the warmth and security of his artificial environment.

Of course, it is possible to suffer minor discomfort and still complete the outing. But when a trip turns miserable, it often affects a person's judgment and compounds minor incidents into major problems. A minor incident such as a person getting lost or confused is a stress situation that requires prudent action immediately, or a person may compound it into a major incident.

Being lost, itself, is only a minor part of a greater problem, that being to stay alive long enough to become unlost. Hence the real problem becomes one of sustaining life, or putting off the hour of death. Man's fear of the unknown blossoms when he becomes disoriented and sees nothing around him that he recognizes. This often allows his imagination to run rampant, causing panic reactions.

Almost every unpleasant outing is the result of many small incidents whose results have combined over a period of time. Not all of these can be anticipated and prepared for at home before the trip. Many of them develop just because of the demands of the trip on the body's energy, muscles, and mind. Often they are compounded by changing weather conditions or terrain difficulties.

Minor physiological problems all post some indicator as a warning that a problem is developing. These indicators often are overlooked or ignored because of inexperience, excitement, or the inconvenience of the moment. Some of these indicators are closely related to other symptoms, resulting in misinterpretation of the warning sign.

How often have you blamed nausea on poor food, when the real problem was the heat and your lack of salt and water? Even the leg muscle cramps you suffer during and after a long, hot hike are blamed upon your lack of body conditioning, when it is really a low supply of salt and other chemical deficiencies. Whenever the body chemistry gets out of balance it quickly gives indications that are warnings that something is wrong. If the condition is not corrected, that particular function of the body will have to slow down or stop.

Body Thermal State Indicators

When man is away from his artificial environment and immediate assistance, the body problem indicators are his only way of keeping a log of the thermal and physical state of his body. Their messages are extremely meaningful to anyone dependent upon a limited supply of energy, water, or body protection to complete a trip successfully. The human body is a chemical machine, very complex, and dependent upon a delicate balance between its components.

The body has many automatic functions and controls which are designed to keep the body, itself, alive, regardless of how man abuses it. When things get too bad, or man fails to assist the body with protective shelter, fuel and water, the body will slow down everything but the brain, breathing, and heart actions. It renders the body incapable of movement until the balance is restored.

Billions of sensory nerves close to the skin surface automatically react to cold and heat. When the skin temperature rises for any reason, they automatically open up the pores and pour water on the skin to cool the skin by water evaporation. The nerves automatically close down the skin blood vessels whenever the skin temperature drops. Prolonged exposure or increasing cold turns the skin numb, then painful, with loss of muscle function ability. Exposed skin is first affected, and the extremities are the first to lose dexterity.

Long exposure to what feels like a mild chill, such as a wind, should indicate that body reserves are being depleted. The counteractions taking place within the body that compensate for failure to protect the body are using up energy, which may limit the enjoyment and travel distance. Wind combined with clothing wetness often cools the body so drastically that the body cannot produce enough heat to prevent accidental hypothermia.

Any portion of the body that is numb from cold is not receiving enough blood to keep the local living cells working for very long. Hence numbness is an indicator of the need for immediate protective covering. The outdoorsman must heed these indicators before the problems become more serious.

COLD INDICATORS AND PROGRESSIVE STAGES

Visible in Self

As over-all skin temperature lowers, mild shivering occurs.
As body core temperature drops, automatic involuntary shivering commences.
Skin chill — mild pain.
Numbness of exposed skin — stinging pain.
Loss of dexterity — inability to move muscles.

Visible in Others

Clumsiness — uncoordinated. Mild shivering.
Hands in pockets, arms and legs held close to body.

Whitish or bluish color to extremities (ears, nose, hands, feet).
Withdrawal from activities — poor articulation — violent shivering.
Irrationality — poor judgment, hallucinations.
White spots on skin indicate frostbite.

HEAT INDICATORS AND PROGRESSIVE STAGES

Heat problems are insidious — they creep up. Often their indicators are not noticed until the combined effect becomes detrimental to the individual. Muscle movement can produce excess body heat, causing the body to over-heat even in a cold environment. Whether the body's overheating is self-inflicted or caused by external heat, excessive body heat causes loss of body fluids and chemicals vital to maintaining proper balance within the body. Sweat-moistened clothing may become a serious problem whenever muscle heat production is stopped or body shelter requirements cannot be met, such as chilling during a rest stop.

Each problem indicator progressively tells its own story of the thermal state of the body. It is the responsibility of the outdoorsman to recognize the signs and to act to prevent their progression. Prompt action is mandatory to offset their debilitating effect.

Visible in Self

Thirst — discomfort. Easy fatigue.
Sweating — body too warm — extremely uncomfortable.
Slowing down of muscle efficiency and capability — frequent rest needed.
Blurring of eyesight — headache. Dry mouth.
Excessive thirst — dehydration.
Painful spasms of voluntary muscles — cramps.
Nausea — sharp, frequent headaches.

Visible in Others

Sweat wetness on clothing
Pinkish skin to redness — sunburn.
Slowing of pace — fatigue. Inability to move muscles — ever more frequent rest stops.
Withdrawal from group — loss of appetite — hallucinations or poor judgment.

Sweating is the body's way of cooling itself. It is normal, but should be analyzed for its total effect on the body. Sweating indicates many things are happening within the body: excessive muscle use; the body's reserves are being used (how long you have sweated will indicate reserves on hand); the fluids (water) are being lost to evaporation; vital body chemicals are being depleted.

This may not be detrimental if supplies are not limited and the environment is serene. The danger situation develops when a person has depleted his body reserves and the weather worsens, or an emergency happens which requires a lengthy stay in these conditions.

Dehydration and Salt Depletion

Water reserves within the body are very limited. Also, water loss causes certain chemical losses that usually upset the body's chemical balance. A combined water loss and chemical loss endangers life primarily by upsetting the nervous system. Body water, in some way, is the conductor or vehicle for nerve impulses. Salt (necessary for chemical balance) fortifies the osmotic action of getting body water into the tissues, glands and vital organs.

Dehydration, or body water loss, is insidious. Often you cannot see perspiration because it is evaporated as fast as it emerges from the sweat glands. On a hot, sunny day, when humans are prone to expose lots of skin, the sun evaporates it before it can bead into a water droplet. A hiker walking in the dry air of the elevations may breath out more than normal water or have it blown away, and unwittingly precipitate dehydration without even feeling overheated.

Body water loss can occur from such a variety of causes that the individual is hard put to analyze where it all goes. Sickness that causes frequent vomiting or a lessened intake of food and liquids, such as seasickness, altitude sickness, or excessive urination or diarrhea, may contribute to the body's water loss.

Drinking excessive amounts of water without intake of carbohydrate food or during a salt deficiency creates a situation where you have a bellyful of water but little water in the tissues and vital organs, where it ultimately is needed, leaving the body with a serious heat problem while full of water.

It is the chemical balance of the system that supports the osmotic action necessary for water to be utilized as a nerve impulse conductor and a body coolant.

Since there are so few clues that show possible dehydration, each outdoorsman should be constantly aware of his own water input vs. possible water losses. The symptoms of water loss nearly parallel other problem indicators, often causing them to be misinterpreted. Only you, the water user, can analyze these symptoms when they occur.

Irritability	Blurred eyesight
Headache	Judgment impaired
Fatigue	Hallucinations
Nausea	Loss of coordination

In areas where available water is minimal if not non-existent, the outdoorsman absolutely must carry more than his expected requirements or be forced to slow down water loss by curtailing heat-producing activities.

Salt Deficiency

Many do not understand how fast a salt deficiency can develop in the weekend hiker, who is unacclimatized to heat. Although we normally maintain our salt balance quite easily through the food we eat, the outdoorsman traveling away from civilization often changes his normal eating habits. Hot environments often lessen the desire for eating, further upsetting the chemical balance so necessary for life.

Salt losses occur whenever the body perspires profusely in an attempt to cool itself. Perspiration and urination are the major sources of salt loss. The outdoorsman travelling on foot often creates excessive amounts of internal heat from muscular action. When internal heat gain is added to environmental heat gain from the sun, the net result will be a water and salt loss that rapidly exceeds the body's minimum tolerance.

Physical indicators of a salt deficiency are muscle cramps in the major muscles in use, accompanied by some nausea, fatigue, headache, and irritability. As soon as the chemical balance is restored, the individual quickly recovers his normal self.

Caution must be emphasized here that salt taken without adequate amounts of water can do more damage than the salt deficiency. Many inexperienced outdoorsmen do not drink enough water with salt tablets. It is the water/chemical balance that allows the body's automatic functions to sustain life. Try to start physical work in hot environments with a water and salt surplus. Your body will excrete the overage. Drink when thirsty, take salt whenever you perspire heavily or you have an abnormal thirst for water that is not satisfied by drinking fluids.

You can and should be able to estimate your water loss from all sources — and thereby estimate your chemical balance. A water or salt or combined water/salt deficiency means muscle and mental troubles.

A dark yellow color of the urine is the early and easily visible sign of a water deficiency. Take heed immediately.

Survival situations can develop anywhere the body can be subjected to stress and thermal problems greater than man's automatic body controls can handle.

Since heat producing activities in a hot environment cause such stress on the body's circulatory system, caution must be exercised by those with heat or circulatory problems. The heart will pump faster to try to move the hot blood from the core to near the skin surface. Also, some of the blood volume is dispersed in the dilated blood vessels near the surface, and not rapidly returned to the heart for recirculation. This problem tends to leave the heart starved for blood to pump. Another factor, gravity, now enters the heat problem. The head normally gets the largest share of the blood supply because of the vital brain and control organs. But the head is two feet higher than the heart, and when circulation volume and pressure is impaired, the head can suffer a depleted supply.

Persons under medication or those with heart problems must use caution in hot environments. The combination of water loss, salt deficiency, and circulatory upset will strain even a physically fit person.

Oxygen Deficiency

Man's living cells oxydize food fuels to produce the energies of life — electrical, mechanical, and osmotic and chemical energies. Without oxygen the cells' functions fail. Even a slight oxygen deficiency can cause a multitude of physiological changes within man's complex bio-electrochemical mass.

Rapid change in oxygen intake can cause physical distress. The outdoorsman today may pick clams from the beaches in the morning and be at 10,000 to 12,000 ft. elevation in the afternoon. People leaving the coast to visit Denver and Aspen will find they have less strength and short breath during the first few days at the higher elevation. Pilots and passengers of light planes often experience this problem in cross-country flying. Such fast transition from dense air to less dense air may create breathing and physiological problems to those who ignore the need for acclimatization. It takes two or three days for the body to acclimatize or adjust itself to the less dense air.

Hypoxia is an oxygen deficiency. The oxygen content of less dense air leaves the body starved for this vital element. Increased breathing and certain blood circulatory responses are the body's first defenses against the deficiency. The higher the elevation, the less oxygen is transferred to the blood hemoglobins. After several hours of a minor oxygen deficiency, you may notice a shortness of breath, dull headache, some abnormal muscle fatigue, and a deterioration of judgment abilities.

In rapid and acute loss of oxygen, such as may happen in depressurization of modern aircraft, or being buried in an avalanche, you will have blurred vision — eyes that do not focus — and possibly euphoria, a false, happy sense of well-being.

Mountain Sickness

Strenuous muscle use in altitudes of less dense air, without time for acclimitization, may cause serious physiological burdens. Mountain sickness is often the result of walking or climbing too fast with an oxygen deficiency. The body must have time to adapt and compensate for this strange environment.

Symptoms of mountain sickness are headache, insomnia, irritability, vomiting, and disturbance of breathing — all in combination or varying degrees, depending upon the altitude, and age and physical condition of the individual.

Recent studies indicate that a low blood sugar level gives similar symptoms and should be considered as a possibility whenever long-term strenuous activity is apparent.

Hyperventilation

It is also possible to get too much of the life-sustaining air, causing another problem called hyperventilation. This can happen when we over-breathe and exhale too much carbon dioxide. When CO_2 level is reduced it changes the blood, causing faintness, dizziness, numbness, tingling, and a pounding of the heart. This overbreathing is usually caused by fear, anxiety, or panic. If recognized it can be easily cured by controlled breathing. The chief danger is that the symptoms may cause further anxiety in the individual affected. Fast treatment — re-breathe exhaled air - via paper bag.

Use of Medication

The human body is often taken for granted while in the proximity of modern technology. It works, it moves, it repairs itself, and it seems that modern medical technology has a pill designed for everything that could go wrong with the body. Many of these simple, everyday pills increase the body's susceptibility to hypoxia, dehydration, and chemical intolerance. Fliers, climbers, hikers and vehicle drivers using medication should read the label and watch for reaction symptoms during travel, especially during heat extremes.

Outdoorsmen, if you want to take pills to cure your minor ills and physical pains, remember — it's not nice to fool Mother Nature, and eventually you will pay for what you get — possibly more than you expected.

Muscle fatigue tells the body that the blood stream is getting clogged with muscle use waste products, and that the demands upon the muscles will have to be slowed down or they will have to cease operations for lack of fresh fuel, oxygen and chemicals. To the aware outdoorsman this means he needs a short rest to clean the blood of some of the accumulated waste products so that the blood can again carry fresh fuel to the muscles.

Pain anywhere in the body is an indicator that something is wrong at that particular point. A blister always starts out as a warm spot in a place that normally is not warm. To prevent a blister, man has to eliminate the cause of the hot spot. Failure to do so results in more pain, until the body automatically puts that body part to rest, stopping the action that created the problem.

Pain anywhere that was not there an hour ago should indicate that something is awry. Even if ignored, as is often possible, it usually continues to try to tell the individual to do something about it. Relieve the cause and symptoms generally disappear.

In major pains, such as broken bones, internal injuries, etc., the body automatically protects the vital organs of the body by rendering the body incapable of further endangering movement.

Regardless of minor pain and the body's problem indicators, man's mind can overrule them. Determination to reach a goal can overrule the fatigue indicators until exhaustion stops all further movement. The mind, or excitement of the moment, can overrule the thirst indicator. Sweat can cool the body only so long before the body exhausts its supply of cooling water. Then the body has no way to cool itself, so it automatically stops the functions that are contributing to the problem.

How man corrects these problems or provides for his body's needs is inconsequential. The fact that he uses any one of the million different ways of helping himself, before the problem compounds itself, insures his body of staying alive a little longer.

ONLY YOU CAN RECOGNIZE THAT YOUR BODY
HAS A PROBLEM

ONLY YOU CAN ACT TO SOLVE THAT PROBLEM

Priorities of Life

Breathing	——————	3 to 6 minutes
Bleeding	——————	3 to 6 minutes
Temperature	——————	3 to 4 hours in extremes

Priorities of Survival

Approx. Length of Possible Survival

1. **Will to live** —— Depends upon you
2. **Oxygen**, or air, for —— 3 minutes
   oxidation of food fuel.
3. **Body shelter** from —— 3 hours
   violent weather and temperature extremes.
4. **Water**, or liquid, for —— 3 days
   body chemistry and cooling while working in extreme heat.
5. **Food fuel** for energy —— 3 weeks

Body Enemies During Survival Emergencies

1. **Your mind,** attitude, determination, imagination, fears, panic.

2. **Injury** — will affect priorities of life and survival. Also may seriously affect mobility, dexterity, coordination.

3. **Temperature** — The body's complex, chemically structured mass of bones, tissues, and muscles, maintains its orderly production of energy within a very narrow temperature tolerance — 95° to 101° F.

4. **Disease.** Germs are present at all times — but are held under control by the body's defense mechanisms, well being, and temperature.

During any emergency
Your body will have a limited supply of

ENERGY . . . WATER . . . OXYGEN . . . BLOOD . . . KNOWLEDGE

PSYCHOLOGICAL STRESS

SURVIVAL A STATE OF MIND

Survival is the challenge to stay alive. Since you have survived long enough to read this, you should have acquired some knowledge about staying alive. How much knowledge about the subject depends upon your curiosity, habits, environment, and input of knowledge. Hence you may or may not have the awareness knowledge necessary to survive a short-term threat upon your life.

Surviving the unexpected emergencies that threaten life is your problem — a problem that, in essence, is yours alone, because unexpected survival problems cannot be planned — they happen. So you must face the problem — with just what you have, where you are — with the sole responsibility for your life resting on your decisions.

No one has to assist you. No one has to find you. No one really has to provide your basic necessities. Even if there are rescuers and agencies nearby who will attempt to help you, you alone must stay alive long enough for them to get to you.

Since you, alone, are master of your destiny, surviving any unexpected emergency becomes your problem to solve. The problem solving can be easy if you know what the problem is, how the problem threatens your life, and how to improvise a defense against that threat.

Some survival emergencies are recognized immediately, such as a downed airplane in the wilderness, or the sudden realization that you are completely lost or disoriented. Other survival situations develop slowly, often without being recognized until it is too late. It is these problems which possess the hidden dangers to life.

When reports of outdoor activity problems are analyzed, it becomes evident that often powerful motivations had a detrimental effect on judgment, mental attitude and the will to live. Evidence shows that these motivations may have even created the emergency situation.

Anything that disrupts normal mental and nervous system control could cause psychological stress or influence physiological reaction and must be considered a threat to staying alive.

REACTIONS TO STRESS

The psychological reactions to any stress situation will vary among individuals, depending upon the type, severity, and location. Familiarity, experience, and knowledge tend to lessen the stress.

Mother Nature has given all animals, people and birds a biological reaction to help adapt to stress situations. The biological changes and adaptations increase the blood flow, supercharge muscle energy, and increase alertness. This is all for one reason — to give you quick reserves to stand and fight when needed, or to run away from danger when the body is threatened.

This adrenal action is short lived and uses tremendous amounts of energy. Several successive scares can leave a person weak and drained, physically and mentally.

THE PSYCHOLOGICAL THREAT TO LIFE

Fears that creep up in wilderness survival situations cause psychological anxieties that often become the greatest obstacles to problem solving and self-control. Fear of the unknown, fear of discomfort, and fear of your own weakness are the most common. There are many more fears that can alter your mental control and affect your survival. Some are even beneficial; others are devastating in maintaining the will to live.

FEAR OF THE UNKNOWN

When an unexpected emergency such as an earthquake occurs, one is startled by the normally solid earth suddenly, and violently moving. Questions flash through the mind: Will the building stand? Do I have time to get out? What if the roof falls? Where is it safe? Will it start again? Will the earth open up?

The mental effect of fear of the unknown can be lessened by recognizing that this fear is a normal reaction. If you expect it to happen, you will be better prepared mentally to cope with the Panic Urge. When you think, "It could happen," you instinctively plan escape routes and think about what you could do. The more you understand how the body functions and what can harm the body, the easier it will be to overcome the fear of the unknown. Training, experience, and practice in testing your ability to cope with strange places and trying situations can be of enormous help in facing the unknowns of an unexpected emergency. Few people practice actual emergencies. But that is what survival training is all about — testing your mental and physical abilities against strange and different situations with numerous variables.

People who are self-reliant and self-confident, who read a lot and possess curiousity, seem to fare the best in unexpected situations. That is one of the major reasons outdoorsmen choose their companions with infinite care. The more you know, the better your chances are of survival.

FEAR OF YOUR OWN WEAKNESS

The second most often encountered mental stress is fear of your own weakness. All too often this fear leads to a do-nothing attitude. When forced to do things that you have never done before, it seems natural to assume some mental anxiety will be experienced.

The mind is a very powerful force — and you are only as strong as you think you are. Self-confidence and the ability to overcome negative thoughts comes from experience in similar situations. Every outdoorsman with any experience can draw upon his storehouse of memories (experienced, read about, or heard) and find workable solutions to his fearful problem. He can tell himself, "This has happened to other people and they made it — if they can do it, I can."

FEAR OF DISCOMFORT

Fear of discomfort probably causes the gravest mental threat in surviving the unexpected wilderness emergency. Modern man is accustomed to comfort and modern technology's instant relief from pain, hunger, thirst, and cold. Fear of discomfort causes people to push on into the storm in

PANIC --
FEAR --

POSITIVE ATTITUDE   *NEGATIVE ATTITUDE*

hopes of reaching the warmth and security of the car, home, or shelter. Generally this mental attitude is concerned with solving the "now" problem rather than solving the real problem of doing what is needed to protect and prolong life.

Naturally, few people relish being cold, wet and miserable. Most survival instructors constantly advise students to make survival camps as comfortable as possible to gain maximum rest. The cramped legs of an improvised emergency shelter may cause temporary discomfort, but at least you may be able to live to tell about it.

The true wilderness abounds with plenty of mud, insects, heat, cold, and other discomforts. Many outdoorsmen have been known to do foolish things to escape their unpleasant effects.

To live, you must tolerate discomfort. Recognize that it is only temporary. Don't let concessions to comfort change your attitude and reasoning. Recognizing discomfort for what it is probably is the best treatment, because it allows the mind to concentrate on effective action to remedy the "real" problem.

HOPELESSNESS

In wilderness emergencies away from civilization, where physical exhaustion or prolonged exposure to cold or heat affects the mind, expect a decline in the will to live. It is sometimes called "give-up-itis" or a passive outlook. But it is seen quite often in strenuous mountain climbs, and has been noted by the survivors of a party lost for days in the woods.

This is a serious condition, which can be noticed by other members of the group, by the unusual behavior of the victim: his withdrawal from the group, loss of appetite, and disinterest in further travel.

Treatment must eliminate the cause of the stress situation. Rest and warmth or cooling if the situation is caused by physical exertion; planned morale building activities by the group if the situation is caused by the loss of the will to live.

A person left alone in such a state of mind may not last long before giving up in total hopelessness.

The psychological threats to a person during and after an emergency situation are a greater problem than most persons wish to acknowledge. In fact, the body ceases when the brain (mind) stops functioning. The brain automatically controls the vital body organs and your mind, with its acquired knowledge, determines where, when and what you subject the body to.

Your self-image will influence your reaction to the stress of wilderness survival situations. Because your sense of values determines the will to live, you have to value life in order to instill the right attitude and to set a goal to live. Positive attitudes have a powerful influence on the morale and motivations necessary for setting a goal to live.

Almost all survivors of short or long term survival experiences at some time set a goal — a goal that was always foremost in their minds. The goal, whatever it was, helped to maintain the fortitude to overcome their physical and environmental obstacles and was the primary preserver of their mental equilibrium. Their goals gave them the motivation and attitude necessary to survive negative pressures.

Self-image can be good or bad for getting out of emergency situations. Consider the plight of a wealthy person who has had little experience in doing anything except eating, sleeping, playing, and spending money. He might have to make as much adjustment to his mental outlook and habits as the young boy or girl who had never had any responsibility but to eat, sleep, play and study. These people develop a dependence upon others to take care of the details of providing their necessities. When faced with a wilderness emergency, all alone, they will be handicapped by their self-image. They lack the needed self-reliance, self-confidence, and the patience to fend for themselves.

Another type of person whose self-image could be detrimental is the one who has a genuine dislike for physical labor other than to push buttons in an office. Such persons not only hate minor physical labor, some are physically incapable of acquiring their necessities if they require any foot travel or strenuous physical effort.

Unfortunately, the cities and homes of our modern society have many of the aforementioned personality types. It is possible one or more may be associated with your survival situation. Look around you; think about your friends, neighbors, and loved ones. Will they be an asset or a detriment during the next emergency?

Suggestions for Controlling Fear in Others:

If you are in a group emergency, fear can become contagious. Every effort must be made to bolster morale and calm the fears, with leadership and discipline. The strength of any group in a survival emergency will be in its ability to work together, and stay together. Inspiring leaders who possess desired attitudes, habits and realistic values generally will demonstrate the self-control and calm behavior that inspires courage in others.

Any one of the ten basic fears can infilter and overcome your will to live. The best defense against group fear is to keep the group occupied with positive action.

Recognize the physical symptoms of fear in others. You may see a teammate trembling, with a strange look in his eyes. He may be talking more than normal, or he may be the opposite — speechless or stammering. He may want to run in panic, or he may be frozen in his tracks. Treat the condition immediately, with calm, reassuring thoughts and physical support, if needed. Use irrelevant talk, that requires answers from the victim. This takes his thoughts off the fear.

In yourself you may notice a quickening or pounding of the heart, sweaty hands and feet, and a funny feeling in the stomach as the body reacts to fright and the dangers that caused it. Treat with mental self-talk and mental pictures of other fearful situations you overcame at another time.

Suggestions for Controlling Fear:

Attitudes and motivation are easily overcome by anxiety and fear. For you to overcome this devastating effect of fear —

1. Expect it, recognize it, and accept the fact that it is a normal reaction.

2. Live with it. Understand how it can alter your effectiveness.

3. Be alert for physical dangers. Recognize potential dangers, then plan several escape routes.

4. Many fears are subdued by keeping the body busy and free from thirst, hunger, pain, and discomfort.

5. Talk to yourself and think positively. Don't let imagination make mountains out of mole hills. Be realistic.

6. Pray. Prayer has, and will continue to be, the most valuable affirmative of staying alive.

Some psychologists suggest that **anger** may overcome **fear.** Anger against that which is causing the fear at least creates a positive attitude to do something, while fear of it creates a defensive or panic attitude. Anger and fear are incompatible. When you feel the quivers and nausea of fear within you, it may be best to get mad and aggressively curse the inconvenience of the situation. Chances are the anger will counteract the fear and allow some rational thoughts and positive actions.

Doctors agree that basic fears do exist, and they acknowledge that under stress man is at the mercy of the mind. These may well be responsible for more deaths than exposure, hunger, or any other danger. FEAR and IMAGINATION plague almost every person who is face-to-face with possible death. Fearfulness that can turn to blind panic may cause an experienced, knowledgeable person to injure or even kill himself in the intensity of his terror.

Realizing that you will have fears and that these are normal emotions in unfamiliar situations, you will be aware of them and better able to cope with them as they appear. Fears can be expected in any survival situation.

Fear of the unknown	Fear of discomfort
Fear of being alone	Fear of suffering
Fear of animals	Fear of death
Fear of darkness	Fear of society
Fear of your own weakness	Fear of personal guilt

The **fear of being alone** can be a very serious emotion, when you think that you may never hear a human voice again. No radio, no companion, nothing but you, alone, against the thousands of unseen things lurking beyond the light of your survival fire. In the realm of unfamiliar environments man is hopelessly at the mercy of the elements and terrain. Loneliness in such situations can become almost unbearable.

The **fear of animals** can be very real to a person in a strange, often foreboding environment. When all alone, let a twig snap in the darkness or a rustling occur in the brush nearby, and even the most experienced outdoorsman will be startled and uneasy. You may know that animals are generally afraid of humans, but add a little imagination to these strange sounds and this nagging, minor fear can turn into terror.

The **fear of darkness** is inherent in most humans. Darkness immobilizes us, blinds us, and hides all familiar things, regardless of the environment. Darkness stirs the imagination and may let it run rampant.

The fear of suffering and death are normal emotions and understandable. No one likes to face suffering, even for a very short time. And the mind and imagination can distort a situation until it can truly become insufferable and perhaps contribute to death.

Fear of Society — Reprisal, loss of face, ridicule — or the fear of inconveniencing or worrying others.

Give-up-itis — Several other aspects of mental attitude must be considered detrimental to humans in survival situations. Give-up-itis is a mental reaction that leads to a do-nothing attitude, which could be the surest way to terminate your life. It represents a complete loss of the will to live, and has occurred even in short-term survival situations.

Panic — The exact opposite of give-up-itis is panic, or the uncontrolled urge to hurry or run from the situation. Panic is triggered by the mind and imagination under stress. At the end of unchecked panic, when all available energy has been used, exhaustion and often death occur.

Knowing that fearfulness and imagination could be a great problem in any survival situation, you are forwarned and can take steps to limit their effect.

Outdoor Recreation's Special Psychological Problems

The factors noted here are carried into the outdoor environment by the recreationist and their combined effect can help to deteriorate judgment and precipitate accidents.

Determination: A state of mind which allows long-sought desires to overrule good judgment. An example of determination is the desire to reach a long-sought, pre-set goal, whatever it may be, regardless of setbacks, storms, loss of equipment or danger to life. This attitude can push a person to use every ounce of energy to attain the goal, leaving none to sustain life during the return journey.

Determination "to do or die" may be a figure of speech, but all too often outdoorsmen will subject their bodies to near impossible tasks under the most severe weather conditions to reach a destination today, when tomorrow or next week the task would be a simple, pleasureable journey.

Promises: This single word quite possibly endangers more lives in our modern society than any other: "Honey, I promise I'll be home in time." "Don't worry, Boss, I'll be to work on time." "I'll be there at 6:00 p.m. sharp." How often have you set yourself a seemingly possible time schedule, only to be delayed? Your promise now creates a stress situation which makes you hurry.

"Haste makes waste." "The hurrier I go the Behinder I get." These are sayings that have proven true in outdoor travel as well as on the highways. To keep promises people have been known to take dangerous shortcuts, run down slippery trails, push on in marginal weather, or travel in darkness. Even risk the lives of companions in an attempt to fulfill their promises.

Every person has responsiblities to himself and to others, and each person assumes obligations which govern his daily life. However, in outdoor travel away from civilization, a person's first and prime responsibility and obligation is to his body — its warmth, its energy and its protection.

Get-home-itis: Another stress factor which can spur a man to disregard the sound precepts of safe outdoor travel. This pressure may be caused by obligations, promises, or even responsibilities that **he feels must be honored** at all costs. In an attempt to honor them he often foresakes good judgment in his decisions in hopes he will be lucky and make it home to relieve these nagging pressures. In a sense his home pressures overrule the common sense actions necessary to sustain and protect his life while away from civilization and immediate help. Outdoorsmen should not underestimate the wrath of an irate loved one. But they must at times consider the worst of the two evils: being late and safety returning home, or pressing on in the face of a storm (instead of finding shelter) and never returning home.

YOUR MIND CONTROLS YOUR SITUATION

The "challenge to stay alive" in hostile environments is a physical and a mental experience to a human. For humans to sustain life in any environment they must have air, body shelter, water and food, and the will to live. These are necessary for sustaining energy production and normal body functions.

How a person may acquire and utilize these necessities to maintain life is determined by the individual's brain. Thus the survivee's brain becomes his greatest asset, or his most dangerous enemy in a survival situation where his life is endangered. When man is forced to adjust quickly from a civilized environment, with all its comforts, to an existence much like that of a cave man, he often develops psychological problems. These are mental problems that can be detrimental to his situation of staying alive.

Energy Use and Loss of Energy — At the onset of your survival situation you will have a limited amount of readily available energy. It may be large or small, depending upon the circumstances before the situation developed. If you were in a plane or vehicle, well fed, warm and rested, you would probably have a large supply of energy available. If you are hiking in hilly or rugged terrain and have been using muscle power most of the day, you may have nearly depleted your available energy supply.

The real challenge to stay alive is to use your brain to conserve this remaining amount of usable energy by limiting your muscle action and by reducing body heat loss. Your situation and actions must be carefully analyzed to determine the immediate and most important needs to improve your chances of living and being rescued.

Often a person must expend energy to travel to a better location to eliminate energy loss due to weather exposure. Energy spent in improving shelter from wind, wetness and cold is energy well spent, because it improves your ability to conserve vital body heat. The challenge is to determine what energy to expend to gain the greatest return for the energy used.

Psychological Fatigue:

"Fatigue" is a term of many meanings, but is basically used to describe those changes of performance that take place over a period of time during which some part of the bodily mechanism gets overloaded. This could be sensory, control, or muscular.

Muscle fatigue is understandable to the outdoorsman, who depends upon his arms, feet, legs and back to carry his body and its necessities in quest of adventure. All too often he overworks these muscles by attempting to travel too far too fast. Tolerable muscle fatigue is good for the total body. It thrives on work. It uses work to improve the cardio-vascular system and respiration, to strengthen muscles, and in general to improve itself.

Only when we travel past the fatigue stage toward the exhaustion stage does it become dangerous to life. In the exhaustion stage the body has a surplus of detrimental waste products and a serious deficit of available and usable energy. Without energy the body's automatic functions deteriorate, threatening the total body.

Most of you reading this book have experienced muscle fatigue at some time during your lives. You have probably experienced other types of fatigue, although the cause may not be quite so obvious.

Mental fatigue causes inattention, carelessness, loss of judgment and reasoning.

Emotional fatigue causes deterioration of normal habits and attitudes.

Sensory fatigue causes disruption of the senses of hot, cold, alertness to danger, etc.

Mental fatigue in outdoorsmen generally results from the monotony of uninteresting travel or confinement because of weather. How do you combat the drudgery of following the seemingly endless footprints in the snow, sand, or "tunnel trail" through high trees? Conquering a summit gives the mind excitement. False summits, fought for at the expense of chronic fatigue and determination, are mentally demoralizing in the light of reality. Nothing seems to demoralize a group quicker than inability to actually see the goal, as in the case of fog, clouds, false summits, or forest. This is one reason being lost is so terrifying. The lost person has lost sight of all goals — the route, the destination, the direction to security, i.e., home, car or camp.

Emotional Fatigue is the other mental stress outdoorsmen should consider whenever in group activity. Some people travel too fast, others travel too slow. Each wishes to travel in *his* personal comfort zone. Each wants the other to change *his* pace. Eventually the unhappy ones vent their feelings. Forced travel in uninteresting environments, such as the "I'll go if you do" wife, or the child that is cajoled into a hike with someone else can be frustrating, disappointing, and lacking in rewards for all participants. Each suffers emotional fatigue that could jeopardize the party's behavior, attitude, and the outcome of the journey. When a small group is traveling together, little things become big things very rapidly. Emotions become tense because of exasperation for the stupidity of others. Mistakes will happen. People are different; they have different attitudes, values, habits. Each has his own personality and behavioral patterns which must be compensated for by the group.

*NOT ALL PEOPLE TRAVEL AT THE SAME SPEED
NOR ENJOY THE SAME THINGS.*

*Remember, children do not recognize fatigue. Often
they travel until they collapse from exhaustion.*

The emotional state of the body is also important because love, hate and fear affect immediate habits, attitudes and motivation, which may affect the body's mental and physical state. Whenever someone is forced out of his personal zone of comfortable actions, he develops a fear of the unknown. Imaginations of failure or embarrassment will cause hesitation or stagefright in the person who is suddenly called upon for performance outside of his accustomed activities.

Everyone has his comfort zone. Some people are leaders, others are followers. Some are players, some are watchers. Whenever an emergency suddenly transfers someone out of his comfort zone, it causes emotional stress.

Sensory fatigue: Some modern men are attuned to noise. Without it they become uneasy. To others, silence is the blessing they search for. However, the steady noise of the incessant wind, roar of big engines, high pitched tone of a whistle, wear on the sensory nerves. Such fatigue affects attitude, habits, and personal values.

To the autoist it may only be center line focus or the monotony of miles and miles of straight road that dulls the senses and slows the body's motor nerve reactors. Hunters, searching for the elusive deer, begin to see horns where no horns are. Their senses become overburdened and the determination and desire increases as the time grows short, until they see horns on anything that moves.

Numbness of skin or fatigue within the extremities of the nerve system disrupts the body's warning and defense mechanisms. Without the feeling and sensory reactions to heat and cold, we may burn hands on hot pots or freeze flesh without realizing it.

Survival is approximately 100% mental because the mind controls the body, its actions and reasoning. Since it is so powerful, we must understand and recognize the conscious level dangers and even consider some of the unusual functions of the subconscious mind.

The Bible says, "As he thinketh in his heart, so is he." The truth in those few words is evident every day. If a man says he feels lousy — he will. If a man says he feels great — chances are he will — all day. The same applies to any given task. If you think it will fizzle, it will. If you are convinced you can do it, more often than not you will succeed.

Some call it positive thinking. Some call it the "can do" attitude. Whatever it is called, you must have it to survive all alone. You will act only as you see your self-image at that moment. If you see your self-image as strong, you will be strong. If you think yourself a weakling, you will be weak. If you think you can't do it, you probably won't do it. If you think you can't survive, you won't try to survive.

Positive thinking is an indispensable asset in improving a difficult situation. It should not be attempted as a substitute for good judgment in selecting a goal.

The subconscious mind is always the mirror of your self-image. It gets its thought fuel from your values, habits and attitude. The subconscious mind is always working and always open for suggestions. Tell a friend that he looks like he has a cold, and chances are he will develop the symptoms. Tell someone that his minor cut will hurt badly, it probably will hurt more than before.

This is nothing new. The Orientals knew about cybernetics thousands of years ago. The power of suggestion has been proven to stop bleeding, make sick persons well, and to make weak people strong. In survival you may have to use this power to do the seemingly impossible, or to keep others with you from becoming non-effective workers.

The conscious level may determine you have a positive need. The subconscious recognizes this thought as a picture and relates that picture to other word pictures and habits previously gained, either positive or negative.

Suppose your subconscious recognizes the input as positive (good), so it passes it on to the creative reality level, along with the related "can do" thoughts needed to solve the problem. At the creative level your positive attitude allows you to try again and again to solve the problem. Each time you fail, you learn what won't work; but your "can do" attitude sees the goal and will solve the problem with time.

The true value of positive thinking rests in the ability to lock out negative thoughts and imaginations that distract from attaining the goal.

The men who have researched this subject put it this way,

> *"The mind can heal the mind,*
> *The mind can heal the body."*

Prayer: Nearly every person who has survived a disaster or serious emergency admits he prayed. Since one's prayers are personal, there is no need to attempt to explain, but only to accept the fact.

Resourcefulness — When survival is threatneed and you have acknowledged the fact that you are scared, you must also acknowledge that you are not helpless. You have many items on your person that can be useful. You have to think like the 20th Century, educated person that you are, but place your thoughts in the caveman's level. After all, the caveman lived in conditions far worse than yours and evolved to what you are today. Think basic needs when searching for the means of keeping warm and dry. Fabric for body shelter, insulation for warmth, metal and wood for shelter from rain and wind.

ADEQUATE shelter is often the key to survival. Many people have preconceived ideas of what a wilderness shelter should be. But in a survival situation one must conserve his limited energy with extreme care. Building an ideal, preconceived shelter may be too costly in energy, as well as insufficient to conserve body heat. Searching for sticks and boughs, lacing them into a shelter, may not be as practical as digging a small, body-sized cave under a downed log, with emphasis on insulation and dryness. The shelter **must provide protection** from convection and conduction of body heat. Your shelter is your home and the most vital part of your survival effort. It can make your survival a comfortable, tolerable wait for rescue or better traveling conditions.

If you are in an airplane, automobile, boat, or near any manmade object when a survival situation develops, stay near these valuable sources of material. Your resourcefulness at improvising your needs can mean the difference between life or death. The thinking man will survive because he recognizes the immediate and most important problem and has the confidence to mentally cope with the problem. Most important, he knows that he must exercise absolute control over all thoughts, imaginations and all physical movement.

In effect, he is living each minute for itself — forgetting the past, concentrating on the immediate problem and the consequences of his actions. The mind plays such a great part in any survival situation that a victim often allows future problems to overshadow the **immediate needs** of living.

Conservation of energy is controlled by the survivee's mind. His knowledge of energy use and loss will determine how long he can make this limited supply last. The mind, and the body with its limited amount of life-sustaining energy, make up the major factors that are prevalent in every survival situation. When either is uncontrolled, the other is sure to perish.

The importance of defensive action cannot be over-emphasized when endeavoring to stay alive under hostile conditions. Mountain Rescue experts rely upon the following when advising what to do in any emergency:

S	Stop
T	Think
O	Observe
P	Plan

S — **Stop.** The body is designed to do three things: digest food, do work, or think. It does not do any two of these very efficiently simultaneously. Hence the need to stop so that you can think. By stopping to think you may avoid the possible errors of hasty decisions.

T — **Think.** Think about the immediate and future danger to self. Analyze the weather, the terrain and the available energy and resources to sustain life.

O — **Observe.** Look around you, observing the problem for possible solutions. Observe resources, weather potential and best possible course of action.

P — **Plan.** After thinking and observing all aspects of your emergency, plan a course of action which will best utilize your limited available energy. Plan your activities, whatever they may be, to take advantage of the natural and ready resources.

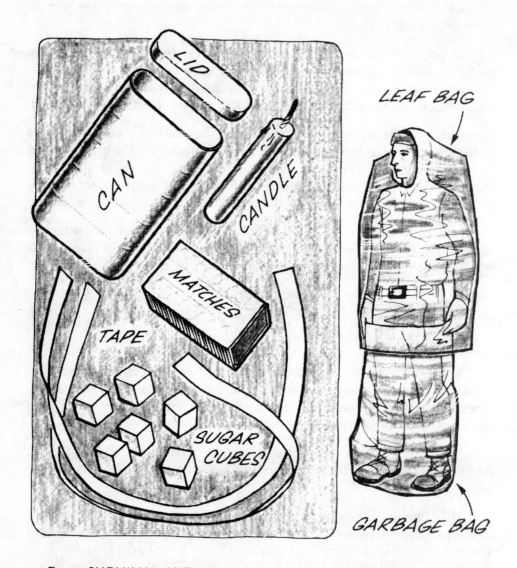

Every SURVIVAL KIT should contain the following items.

A means of instant body protection from the elements.
A means of instant energy to help sustain the body.
A means of carrying and heating water for internal warmth.

5 ∘ ∘   GENERAL SURVIVAL

GENERAL PROBLEMS OF SURVIVAL

Many survival books expound on the general problems of living off the land in foreign places, such as the frozen Arctic, burning desert, or the steaming jungles. Often they assume the survivor will always have special equipment, clothing, and the basic knowledge or common sense to get through the first 24 hours of the emergency. Only a few of them look at survival in respect to everyday living emergencies.

These books about long-term survival (over five days) are good, and the survival training they support is excellent for the global traveler, who may travel over these extremely hostile lands and someday have to set snares and traps, search for wild foods, and dig for water, to stay alive. But the point to remember is, you have to live long enough to set the snares, search for food and water by daylight. Accident and rescue reports show

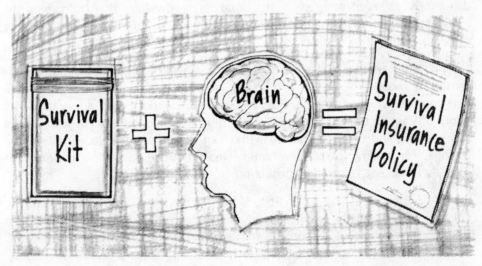

that a surprisingly large number of would-be survivors could not stay alive long enough in moderate temperatures to even hunt for food. And some could not survive even with food, shelter, and water, in a non-hostile environment. Hence the need for more knowledge about short-term survival (from two minutes to five days) based on the assumption you have nothing but the clothes you wear and the surrounding environment, whatever it is.

Your survival is a problem not only in the Arctic, desert or jungle; it can happen anywhere. It is simply keeping the body alive long enough to get out of a body-threatening predicament. To put survival into meaningful perspective, think of it this way "If you wake up in the morning, you have survived the night." Survival is staying alive — anywhere, any time — at home, office, driving, hiking, climbing, swimming, boating, flying, eating, sleeping and doing anything else people do.

Unfortunately, our modern, mechanized society has created a fast-moving and potentially dangerous environment wherein a threat to your survival may develop in the next second or around the next corner. Few modern Americans are really convinced that they will ever need wilderness survival education. Few ever expect to have to live by Nature's rules in an environment that is hostile. And very few expect to ever be without electricity, running water, warm homes, and grocery stores.

To understand why wilderness survival emergencies are serious and dangerous to everyone, even the apartment dweller, it would help to understand what constitutes a wilderness emergency. Most of us have been close to one — too close.

If you have ever driven a car across a desert in the heat of summer, or crossed a mountain pass in a blizzard, no doubt you recognized the value and comfort of your vehicle. Possibly you even experienced a few thoughts about "What if the car stalled?" If it did, you had an emergency. Things can happen, and often do happen, that can leave you stranded or alone in a strange, foreboding place. Mechanical malfunctions cause the majority of today's unexpected survival problems.

A wilderness is, by definition, (1) an uncultivated, uninhabited region, (2) any barren, empty or open area, as an ocean, (3) a large, confused mass of people or tangle of persons or things, (4) a wild condition or quality.*[1]

1.   Webster's New World Dictionary of the American Language, The World Publishing Company, 1954.

A child lost in the forested park, or an Eskimo stranded on the desert, would face strange and frightening obstacles. To them those strange places are not unlike a wilderness full of unexpected dangers.

A wilderness emergency could happen just about anywhere a person suddenly loses those things he relies upon for comfort and security, which in our day could be the loss of modern technology and the accompanying service industries. An earthquake, flash flood, tornado, tidal wave, or electrical outage — all have a way of disrupting the normal supply of the energy that powers the modern technology of your home, office, automobile. A city without electricity quickly becomes cold, jobless, and inhospitable. Once your home or auto has become cold, the insulation reverses its function and now keeps the cold in and the heat out. Without fuels, cooking becomes a major problem. The service industries you depend upon now all slow down operations; some even stop. People become uneasy and fearful. Habits must be changed and new ones adopted just to cope with this emergency that forces you to immediately change your life style. The bigger the city, the greater the dependence upon purchased goods and services, the more vulnerable the individual is upon the interruption of electricity and other utilities or of service industries.

When a city dweller, wholly dependent upon the service industry, suddenly loses it, he must live by Nature's rules. To you experienced outdoorsmen, this would be the equivalent of being suddenly put high on a windy mountain without the benefit of any physical or material preparation for the trip.

If you are one of those who thinks it cannot happen to you because you do not climb high mountains, travel in jungles, deserts, or Arctic snow nor hike in the woods, think again. It could happen as you read this. Natural or manmade disaster usually strikes unexpectedly. Look around you right now. Could you get to safety in an earthquake? What if it happened tonight on the way home by auto, train, or plane. Could you remain comfortable with the clothing you now wear? What about bridges, roads — would they be usable? In fact, could you get home?

Since survival is keeping your body alive, there are general problem areas that develop in both short-term and long-term body threat emergency situations, anywhere. The personal threat of body harm is the same for the man lost in a mountain wilderness during a storm as it is for the man watching his valley home float away in the storm-born flash flood. Each is exposed to the same wind, rain, and cold. Each must combat the urge to panic. Each must think and seek some type of body protection immediately. A person walking home from the office in such a storm also is exposing his body to abnormal conditions that take away heat faster than the body can produce it.

THREATENING PROBLEMS

You can expect certain problems to occur in all body-threatening emergencies that incapacitate or immobilize you. The major problems that present themselves in most survival emergencies fall into four groups:

Mental control and solving the immediate problem.

Caring for injuries and mental stress.

Sustaining and protecting the body.

Signalling your distress and location.

MENTAL DANGERS IN SURVIVING EMERGENCIES

Whatever causes your emergency and the problems of staying alive, chances are your greatest problems will be mental. Coping with the immediate danger while planning acquisition of future necessities requires realistic thinking. You cannot afford reliance on plans, promises, or dependence upon hopes. For the immediate time you are on your own and sole master of your actions and destiny. You may have to make life or death decisions. Those unable or unwilling to make decisions for themselves will have to rely upon the judgment of others — if they are available.

MENTAL CONTROL

Surviving the unexpected short-term emergency will be problem solving. Solving one problem at a time, living each second and each minute. Staying alive by using acquired knowledge to solve the most pressing and immediate problem until you are safe and secure.

IMPROVISE, IT'S YOUR LIFE!

In case vision is blurred because of loss of your eye glasses you can manage to distinguish single world small print by focusing the eye through a pin hole in paper, or the slit between pinched fingers held close to the best eye.

Think. Your brain is your best survival tool. Remember those words, because they calm the fears and spark the will to live. Talk to yourself. Visualize by psycho-pictography what your immediate action should be. Look ahead; see how you might look in an hour if you do what you plan to do. Talk to yourself about the future consequences of the planned action. Think ; plan; visualize the results — then act out the plan.

EVALUATING CIRCUMSTANCES

There are few mistakes allowed in a serious body threat emergency. It is the little mistakes and misjudgments that often cost your life. At times, every step must be carefully planned. Every plan should have an alternate plan because any plan could be interrupted by unexpected events. And any plan is only as good as your physical ability to carry it out safely amid the environmental hazards at the time.

A cut finger or a broken leg poses only minor problems if hospital care is immediately available. The same cut or broken leg could be a survival problem fifteen miles into the back country.

Solving the body threat problem and improvising your immediate necessities may seem impossible in the light of the circumstances of your emergency. But you have to understand the problem, its scope and serious-ness, before you can ascertain the priorities of action. Some emergencies happen so quickly and are so dangerous you must rush to find safer ground. Others allow time to analyze and plan.

Do first priority things first. There is little point in stopping severe bleeding as your head sinks below the water and your supply of life-sustaining air is cut off. That is why all survival instructors stress, "Find out what the real problem is and the solution is generally simple and easy to see and improvise. Think realistically. Think priorities of need. Do first things first.

Never knowingly place yourself in a situation where you have no control of your fate. It's your life, and only you are master of it and in control of it.

MENTAL OBSTACLES

Curb the urge to panic. Your mind and its storehouse of lessons learned (by listening, reading, practice, or experience) can instill the confidence to succeed. The more decision-making experience, the better your chances are of controlling the mind and solving the problem.

Mental obstacles such as fear of the unknown are experienced by almost everyone. They can be overcome by understanding what can harm you and how it may harm you. Once you know the enemy you can try to dispell the fear of it. Fear of your own weakness will be much harder to overcome unless you have had some previous experience in living alone and creating things with your mind and hands. If you experience fear of your own weakness you may have to rely upon mental pictures of how others you have seen on T.V. or read about, overcame a similar obstacle. Think of all similar situations you yourself have conquered. Even non-similar incidents you conquered can bolster confidence to do something needed. Once you do something that works, by using the "think power" you become confident that knowledge will produce more usable solutions.

Imagination can be a great help in improvising your necessities, or it can get you into deeper trouble by contriving complications to your real problems. Those "What if I can't" thoughts really discourage any attempt to do anything to improve your situation. Think positive. Dispell any negative thoughts immediately. It is mandatory that you do something to improve your situation.

If you are uninjured, with a good mental attitude, and in relatively good health, you can survive a severe short-term emergency just by maintaining and controlling the inner and outer environments of your body. But it takes mental control and recognition of body priorities and body enemies to improvise the needed body protection.

Throughout this book you will find repeated reference to mental control. This is not intended to add pages to the book, but because the mind is directly involved in everything you do or think about doing.

Material things that cannot and will not contribute anything to help you stay alive are burdens, and may become a millstone around your neck. Carrying cameras, broken guns, souvenirs, a heavy stove without fuel, etc., may waste vital energy. Keep everything useful. Discard only the nonessentials.

TRAVEL AFTER AN EMERGENCY

Your fears may urge you to run from a scary place. Imagination may envision indescribable horrors pending. Sort out the real from the unreal. Don't run unless the threat is real. You must consider your safety at all times. Be realistic in decisions to travel. Travel takes time and body energy. All travel decisions must consider the environmental dangers, water and energy depletion, shelter, signalling capability during the trek. (This applies to freeway and city problems during certain hours.)

No one should attempt to travel until he is sure of where he is and where he is going. Wandering aimlessly only depletes your limited supply of life-sustaining energy. Any foot or vehicle travel requires a means of determining and maintaining a direction — compass, stars, sun, signs, maps, trail, road, etc.

Except to move out of the path of danger, no one should travel immediately after a threatening emergency. Your body is charged with the adrenalin for high speed activity at the time of the emergency. Superhuman feats can be accomplished, if necessary, during this very short time span. But expect a fatigue-like letdown later. Within a few minutes, the emotional upset of the emergency creates a mental and physical shock which lasts approximately two hours. If you are in a safe location, hole up and allow this extreme shock to subside.

Stay put if you are near manmade materials usable in improvising immediate shelter and to signal your distress.

GROUP SURVIVAL

A common threat, or danger that threatens a group, will present a multitude of problems, moods, attitudes and emotions. In group survival it is mandatory to elect a strong leader, to organize work, plan, delegate responsibilities, determine necessities, strengthen morale, with the prime goal to keep the party together. The real strength of the group is in its leadership and the ability to support one another mentally, emotionally, and physically. Organization is the key to group survival. Organize action, using the personnel best suited for the job, when possible, keeping everyone busy improving the group's situation. Equipment pooling, food and water rationing must be considered if resources are limited. Be aware that any dissention or negative attitude may disrupt the total group effort. The leader who is dictatorial and unreasonable is apt to be faced with the additional problem of an insurrection of the group. Discipline with a dedication for all to live is the best rule to follow in any group emergency.

CARING FOR
INJURIES and PHYSIOLOGICAL/PSYCHOLOGICAL STRESS

SURVIVAL MEDICINE

Any outdoorsman walking away from the instant relief from pain offered by modern medicine and immediate response of medical doctors and hospitals, should know enough first aid to patch up his own body until help can arrive. Survival medicine implies more than first aid; in survival all alone, it is necessary to help yourself or perish. Your rescuers may take minutes, hours or days to reach you, depending upon your distance from them and your ability to signal your distress.

GENERAL MEDICAL PROBLEMS

Your general health has much to do with your ability to recover from severe diseases or injuries. Your knowledge of body functions, body problem indicators, will help you to determine the seriousness of the injury and the action needed to prevent infection and more danger or damage.

Since nearly all of the body processes use water, water becomes even more important to sustain life during any injury or disease caused fever. Water flushing and cleanliness are the prime treatment for all injuries involving wounded skin. Cleanliness is essential to prevent infection. Infection of even the small cuts and scratches can affect your chances of surviving.

Prevention of injury and thinking of consequences before acting is by far the best rule for staying healthy. Treatment of injuries caused by stupid mistakes or miscalculations in emergency situations only increases your burden of responsibility.

BLEEDING

Control of bleeding is necessary to stop the loss of this vital fluid. Elevation of the injured part, or direct pressure are effective means of stopping venous and minor arterial blood flow. Major arterial blood flow from serious injuries requires pressing the artery against a bone. Knowledge of pressure points and simple bandage procedures should be in every outdoorsman's storehouse of knowledge.

PAIN

Pain and shock accompany all injury. They are difficult to treat in emergency situations. Pain influences mental shock and contributes to physical shock, making your more vulnerable to other problems.

Pain is your nervous system telling you that something is wrong somewhere. The best treatment is to eliminate the cause, if possible. Controlling the pain may be possible by putting the part that is hurting to rest. Supporting splints, bandages, immobilization or elevation may help. Cold or heat can help certain injuries, inflammations, bruises, body aches, burns. Remember that pain can be overruled by determination and the necessity to move from a more serious threat. You can move if you have to.

SHOCK DANGERS

Shock will occur to some degree with all injuries. It may be the most serious consequence of the injury. Don't wait for symptoms to show in the victim. Expect them to occur. Treat for shock in all injured persons. Even in non-injury emergencies, the mental trauma may be such that a person will experience mental shock. Treat mental shock the same way as injury shock. It takes only a little time, warmth, and rest to prevent an immobilizing setback later.

Shock is caused by a serious upset of the blood circulation to the vital organs (especially the brain) which supply and control your body. The best treatment is rest in a supine position with the head slightly lower than the body's trunk. The one exception will be a head injury, where the head must not be lower than the body. Blood supply to the brain is mandatory for the brain's control of the body's physical and mental functions. Keep the victim warm but not too hot until the pulse is strong and normal. Do not attempt to travel until the victim's eyes are alert, attitude normal, and the skin is warm again.

If you are alone during a serious emergency, plan on shock hitting you within minutes following the emergency, even if you have no injuries. Expect it. If unable to lie down with head lower than feet, sit down in a safe place, head between your legs. Put on warm clothing. Rest for as long as necessary to allow your body to readjust the blood flow to the brain.

Shock can occur to persons losing body fluids through excessive, prolonged sweating, vomitting, or diarrhea. Suspect shock to follow any problem that could upset the body's volume/capacity ratio of the blood circulatory system, because lack of blood flow to the brain is a serious threat to the total body.

INJURY TO BONES

Generally, the victim will be aware that something is broken because of the accompanying pain at the site. Possibly the sound of a snap from the site, and immediate loss of power to the limb.

Treatment must be to immobilize the limb to prevent further injury to the bone and surrounding tissue. If medical assistance is not expected for a long time, an immediate effort to align the bone before splinting should be attempted. Gentle stretching of the limb often allows the surrounding tissue and muscles to realign the broken ends. It will be less painful if done immediately, and will hasten recovery of minor broken bones.

Broken bones that break the skin require special treatment for both the bone and the wound. Immobilize in a manner that allows treatment and cleaning of the open wound.

WOUNDS

The seriousness of the wound will be determined by its location, size, possible contamination, and amount of blood loss. Expose the wound. Stop blood flow. Use clean water to irrigate the wound, if deep or contaminated. Once the extent of the wound is determined, clean the surrounding skin with soap and water; cover with a bandage as sterile as can be obtained.

Do not travel unless the injury can be immobilized to prevent recurring bleeding and pain. The prime goal is to stop blood loss and keep the wound clean and free of infection until proper medical attention can be obtained. Ointments, oils, or strong tissue-burning antiseptics are not recommended because they tend to retard normal tissue healing.

If medical aid is not expected for a long time due to distance to civilization, attempts must be made to close large, deep cuts that are caused by relatively clean instruments such as axes, knives, etc. Butterfly adhesive tape ties will hold most cuts closed. Sewing the cut shut with a needle and white thread might be used in a desperate situation. Use a sterile needle and the single loop and its method.

Deep or large cut

Make ends long | For maximum holding power

Pinch skin tight together

BURNS

The pain from any type of extensive burn causes shock. Shock, loss of body fluid, possible skin infection, and skin loss, are the dangers in burns. Prevention is far better than a cure, and far less painful. But the burn should be treated quickly. Don't walk to the water, Run! To take away the heat, immediate immersion in cool or cold liquid can reverse the action of the heat penetrating to deeper tissue.

TREAT ALL BURNS WITH COLD ANYTHING.
To draw away the heat before it can
damage the deep tissue.   BE QUICK!!!!!

If large areas are burned from sunburn or a clothing fire, expect shock and severe pain, which will require continuous reassurance and T.L.C. Expect dehydration and salt deficiency. If you are one or two days away from civilization and medical aid, medicate with any sterile ointment that reduces the pain. Some severe cases may require artificially cooling the victim.

The serious danger from burns, especially large area sunburn, is the loss of performance of the sweat glands in the burn area. Whenever you lose the functioning capability of a large number of your sweat glands, you lose the body's ability to cool itself automatically. This can cause a multitude of related problems: Shock, dehydration, fluid and chemical imbalance. Then the problem will be that you will have to be cooled artificially with wet cloths. This is not easy to do if you are alone.

BURN FIELD TREATMENT:

Cover area with wet soft cloth (several layers). Cover wet cloth with clean sheet plastic (tape snug to body). Seal edges with wide tape. This keeps area moist, clean and air-free. (Keep cloth moist during evacuation.) Medical ointments, fat, oils, grease used to keep air from burn may be covered with plastic to prevent saturation and chaffing. Administer salty water frequently. Unconscious burn victims can absorb salt tablets placed behind lower lip.

Your body has amazing recuperative capabilities if you give it a chance by resting. The healthy body repairs itself. The pills and medication taken internally and externally generally help to rest the body, relax the tension, and calm the mind or help to prevent infection from outside contamination. Their prime purpose is to calm your mind so the body can get on with the job of repairing itself. Even pain can be controlled with positive, pleasant, distractive thoughts. Self treatment for minor — and even major — injuries or medical problems is mandatory before the body becomes debilitated from the after effects of the problem.

BOREDOM

The lack of interest is considered a form of mental fatigue which must be relieved to maintain a healthy survival attitude. It can be accomplished in many ways, from diversification of work, to daydreaming.

To modern day T.V. enthusiasts, boredom is relieved by instant channel change. But boredom can become a major problem during a five-day storm that keeps you confined to a small snow cave or two-man tent. In sitting out the storm, do everything possible to prevent tent fever. Sleep, play games, solve mental problems, plan a year of fun. Don't let the boredom goad you into attempting foolish travel.

LONELINESS

This may be one of the more critical problems of surviving all alone. Self-sufficient persons who enjoy problem solving usually can manage being alone. But modern society gives little chance to test your ability to adapt to silence, loss of support, separation from loved ones, or the drastic change and fury of hostile environments. Being self-sufficient is something everyone must learn by doing: attempting, exploring, and facing problem solving head on. Self confidence and self reliance are the major benefits from any attempts to conquer the fear of loneliness.

The emotional ties that run deep and strong among families and lovers can cause anxieties that influence loneliness. They must be controlled to prevent get-home-itis. Loneliness may cause a different kind of problem for the one who does not have such strong home ties, as he may tend more toward a case of give-up-itis.

FAMOUS LAST WORDS

"I wish I hadn't
left my pack
in the car."

Much of our daily life is regulated by how we feel mentally. If we feel physically and mentally well, chances are the day will be good. The reverse is equally true. The Bible says, "As he thinketh in his heart, so is he." Man normally will act only as he sees his self-image at that moment. Man's self-image is basically determined by his habits, values, and attitude. And habits, values and attitudes are directly related to and influenced by the person's mental, physical and emotional state.

SUSTAINING AND PROTECTING THE BODY

THIRST

Thirst always seems to be the most noticeable and feared of survival emergencies. Once the body demands fluid replacement, the body starts to take the necessary fluid from reserves stored in the body. Enough loss of these reserves will cause you to experience a dry mouth and a thick tongue. The blood will become thick and the nervous system loses its response speed.

Most Americans take water for granted, because we acquire it from so many varied ways. We forget how necessary it really is until we fail to carry it or are denied it. Also, psychologically, you become thirsty whenever your canteen is empty. Likewise, in the city you become thirsty when the faucet does not flow water.

Salt/water management is necessary to keep the body at normal efficiency, and must be considered vital to your survival any place you walk away from civilization and modern technology's services, or any place that is deprived of these services by natural or manmade disaster.

The body does not care where it gets its water — from fruits, juices, meat, vegetables, pop, or plain water. Alcohol can hasten dehydration. Only water in some form will prevent the debilitating effects of dehydration.

Among the many ways you can lose water faster than normal are from fever, sweating, overwork, diarrhea, vomitting, and exposure to evaporation.

Ironically, dehydration or water loss and accompanying salt/chemical deficiency, often does not give any warning signs. Sweat is silent and not painful. Sweat often evaporates before a water bead can form on the skin to indicate its presence. Those without clothing on hot days seldom recognize that they are sweating and dehydrating until the debilitating effects begin to show.

Remember, no one but you can manage your body water/salt balance. Management is accomplished by mentally weighing all intake of salt and water against the total output or loss by all the many ways.

RATION YOUR SWEAT . . . NOT YOUR WATER

HUNGER

Food fuel, like water and oxygen, is necessary to sustain the lifegiving cells within the body. The physical effects of hunger during a short term emergency generally are more psychological than real. However, the extent of physical activity determines how fast energy giving fuels are depleted. Physical exertion requires more food fuel, water, and oxygen. Since your resupply of food fuel may be curtailed during your emergency, it may be mandatory to limit energy expenditure.

The real danger is mental. Most moderns are used to the instant relief from hunger pangs and all the comforts of a full belly. Some can endure hunger, others think they cannot. If you are healthy and comfortable you should last at least two to three weeks without food — not enjoyably, but tolerably.

We have largely avoided the subject of searching for natural foods, for a specific reason. This aspect of survival has been so emphasized by our overfed society that a person faced with an emergency is apt to abandon all concern for his more urgent body necessities while he concentrates on food procurement. We actually read the account in the local newspaper of a boy, lost overnight in the woods, attributing his survival to the fact that he had spent the night wading around catching polywogs to eat. Of course, the newspaper made no attempt to evaluate the logic of this method of survival. We would like to suggest that since getting cold and wet was much more life threatening than going without supper, he survived in spite of his training, not because of it. (However, the very fact that he had been told what to do, and he had confidence that it was the right thing, probably saved him from panic, which could possibly have been even worse than getting wet.)

Natural food is abundant in most green areas. The problem becomes one of immediate knowledge of what is edible, what is poisonous, and what is worthless. Such information has been omitted from this text because of the variable growth habits of edibles and their seasonal, territorial, and climatic limitations.

Since food is the least important of your needs and priorities during short term emergencies, it did not warrant the words necessary to familiarize the reader with selecting, picking, preparing, and cooking.

FATIGUE

Physical and mental fatigue become a serious threat to survival whenever they cause a careless attitude, frustration, or hopelessness. Fatigue is the result of overuse of muscles or mind,   Mental fatigue may be caused by forced inactivity. The gravest danger is when muscle fatigue immobilizes you in a dangerous location. Remember that YOU CAN muster temporary strength to get to a safe location. But rest is the only way the body's automatic controls and functions can cleanse the body of fatigue-causing waste products. Pep pills and medications that mask the body's problem indicators only cause the fatigued person to walk a little farther before totally collapsing.

The body is a truly fantastic machine. It can keep traveling for days and days, or it can perish in hours. It really depends upon the will and determination of the mind.

FATIGUE IS . . .

Moving muscles too fast.

Set a pace that the heart and lungs can tolerate.

Fatigue is your body's problem indicator telling you that you are moving too fast and not conserving your limited energy supply.

SLEEP

The body must have sleep and rest to rid itself of the accumulated waste products of energy use. However, sleep does not have to be eight hours long, nor flat out in a bed. Cat naps of an hour or so often can get you through a short term emergency. Rest can be more beneficial if you collapse and rest all muscles rather than lean against a tree. It takes mental control to relax and rest all the muscles. Some of you reading this are tense. Try to relax. Notice the tense muscles needed to sit and read.

Take advantage of darkness, when you are generally immobilized, to acquire sleep and rest. Concessions to comfort, shelter, warmth, will enhance the quality of sleep-rest you receive. This is generally considered energy and time well spent.

Rest whenever you can. Enjoy the moment of rest. Give the mind a rest from the stress of the emergency. Enjoy the beauty of the spot in which you are resting. Nature had made the landscape beautiful just for you and your moment of rest. Enjoy it.

COLD AND HEAT

Both of these common enemies may affect your short term emergency. Heat because you are an automatic heat producing machine; cold because you may be in a cold, wet, or windy environment. Both have a way of insidiously causing detrimental effects within the body that can affect your mobility and ability to solve your immediate problems.

The dangers and effects of heat and cold are extensively covered in the appropriate chapters of this text. Study them carefully, because they can become the most serious threat to life in any emergency.

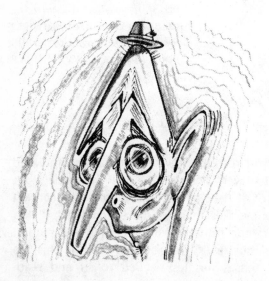

Often the challenge to stay alive is man against himself. It is his unending struggle to control the mind and alleviate discomfort while improvising his ever-pressing needs and improving his chances of acquiring assistance.

In certain climates you will be exposed to considerable heat and must safeguard yourself from its effects. While the body will adjust to heat, the process takes time, and you must be especially careful during the first period of your exposure.   First 2 days are critical .

In other climatic extremes the problem of cold injury becomes proportionately important. Cold injury is much better prevented than treated.

Clothing and body shelter is undoubtedly the most valuable asset in a survival situation. The protection it offers the body from hostile elements determines the degree of discomfort and danger to life a person will experience.

Along with all of the heat, cold and wetness dangers and discomforts, man may also have to contend with an insect problem. During the summer many areas have flies, mosquitos, no-see'ems, and other seemingly ferocious flying insects. Some really bite, some sting, and some are everywhere — in the eyes, ears, nose and mouth. Some stings cause skin swelling and irritations, others cause only mental agony.

Insect repellents offer some relief, but the best protection is complete covering — clothing and netting which stand out away from the body. In some areas, like the arctic tundra, alpine meadows and moist jungles, the flies and insects bite right through clothing. These flying pests may create only a minor discomfort, or they may goad you into actions that will complicate your survival situation.

MENTAL CONTROL

The patience to sit within the confines of your cramped emergency shelter is born of your ability to control your mind and subdue your urgent desire to travel towards home. The pain of cramped muscles, cold bottom, numb toes, empty stomach, dry mouth, and biting insects constantly remind us of the discomfort of the shelter, this place, this moment. Our discomfort interrupts our enjoyment of the life-sustaining shelter from the howling wind, penetrating wetness, and finger-nipping cold. Let us not forget the positive and let the negative monopolize our thoughts and possibly influence our movement and motivations.

Too soon you may forget that the shelter is a blessing that is saving your life. Pain and discomfort are only the body's way of telling you to improve the shelter, the situation, and eliminate the irritant.

If you can mentally see the positive blessing of the moment and enjoy it for what it really is, your body and the 639 muscles that hold it together can tolerate the discomfort.

Mental control can:
Warm your hands and feet by concentration on increase of blood flow.
Reduce pain and even eliminate it.
Reduce blood flow to injuries.
Subdue negative thoughts, fears, and imaginations.
Contract all or any one of your large muscles for confined space exercise to reduce stiffness.
Get an unpleasant job done.

COMMON SENSE

In the records of survival situations, some victims managed much better than others faced with similar circumstances. This was not always because of one being stronger or better prepared. More often it was because one had more common sense. Common sense, or ordinary good sense, is something that land management people hope all outdoor recreationists will someday acquire. Foresters and Rangers maintain that common sense could alleviate many of the wilderness emergency problems. Everyone hears about common sense. But what is it, and how can the inexperienced acquire it? A study of outdoorsmen adjudged to have common sense indicates that they all had certain basic human attributes:

They understand the priorities of life and survival.
They can recognize and analyze body problem indicators.
They can recognize a danger problem developing.
All are curious, inquisitive, alert, confident, and search for information.
They can apply sound judgment to time and environmental problems.
They are decisive after analysis of the problem or threat.
They enjoy a mental or physical challenge.
All are seemingly non-destructive of material things; most are do-it-yourselfers, and work well alone.

Notice that every one of the above list involves the mind and acquired values and attitudes.

Signalling distress

Signalling your distress and location probably will be the most important factor in getting assistance. Staying alive long enough to be able to signal is, of course, the prerequisite. But if you do not signal your distress, and the location thereof to others, you may spend considerable time trying to stay alive without assistance.

Signalling your location is a must priority . Certain types of signals indicate distress, and most unusual signals are investigated by those curious persons who hear and see them. Signals are a means of making yourself effectively bigger (more conspicuous), and the better your signal, the quicker someone may see it.

Many types of signals are available, such as radios, flares, panels, lights, mirrors, noise, flags, markers, writing, fire, smoke. What types you have available, the time of day, and circumstances will determine your actions. Use as many types as possible during the best times they may be seen.

To get the most out of your signals:

Know how to use the signals.

Have them ready for use.

Be careful with flares and fire and dangerous signals.

Survival emergencies involving modern, man-made equipment will give you a multitude of materials that can serve as signals.

Smoke and fire are the most noticeable of all signalling methods during daytime. Use dark or black smoke against light colored background. Plastic, oil, fabric, wire insulation, tires, or rubber mats burn quite rapidly and make dark colored smoke. Dust clouds or brush lettering utilize the same thinking of contrast between signal and background.

Contrast is the key for effective signals, especially if you are trying to signal search aircraft. Moving flags of bright colored material are more easily seen than non-moving flags. Use every available means to make your plight known to others. Color your white airplane if you are down in the snow or white sand. Make white or light colored smoke by putting moss, green boughs or grass — or sprinkle water — on a hot fire.

Wear contrasting colored clothing in the forest. Learn how to use such signals as a mirror and radio transmitter. Proficiency in their use could lessen the length of your emergency.

MIRRORS

The small flash of brilliant light can be seen for miles during sunlight. In fact, it is so bright that rescue pilots have complained of being blinded by overzealous survivors on the ground. Such a mirror can be made from almost any shiny metal. The use is simple, yet extremely effective in open, sunlit areas. But you have to know how to use it — see page 76. Then go out and practice the technique until proficient. Once you have learned something, by reading and doing, it will be usable when you need it.

The little ant in the grass is hard to see. But if he waved a yellow flag and flashed a mirror in your eyes, you might see him.

The moral of this cartoon is

When you are in the forest or brush land, you are just as hard to be seen by airplanes searching for you. Signals make you effectively bigger.

SHADOW SIGNALS

Shadow writing with brush, boughs, rocks, or piles of snow and dirt can tell of your plight. Place them so they get the maximum effect of shadow. Large letters tramped in the snow can be seen from great heights. The simpler and larger the letters, the more easily understood.

S.O.S. are the universal letters used to indicate "I need help." Since they are recognized by all, it would be wise to use these letters for your shadow signals. Other simple, easier to make, air-ground code letters are listed on Page 164.

If no open area is near your distress area, disturb the vegetation so it looks unnatural. Tramp down a large area of brush in a triangle, or cut or bend over giant marker lines in small, dense forest or brush land. Most observers searching from an airplane will look at your general area once or twice for approximately three seconds during a fly-by. To attract his attention, have signals ready for instant use as he approaches you. He will be looking ahead and to the side of the aircraft, not behind. So if he has gone past, save your signals and hope he returns past your area.

For other means and methods of signalling, read the chapter on improvising. Remember that signalling your distress is necessary even in our modern cities, and may become absolutely essential in serious natural disasters, such as earthquakes, tornados, flash floods, etc. Here the same signalling rules apply. Contrasting color, sounds, flashes, or moving flags help attract the attention of others.

Think! You can solve the problem and you can improvise a means of telling others of your distress. Try anything and everything during the best possible time for them to be seen, heard, or felt.

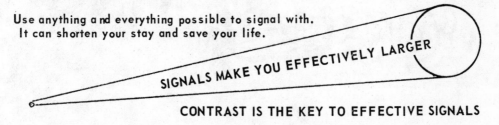

Use anything and everything possible to signal with.
It can shorten your stay and save your life.

SIGNALS MAKE YOU EFFECTIVELY LARGER

CONTRAST IS THE KEY TO EFFECTIVE SIGNALS

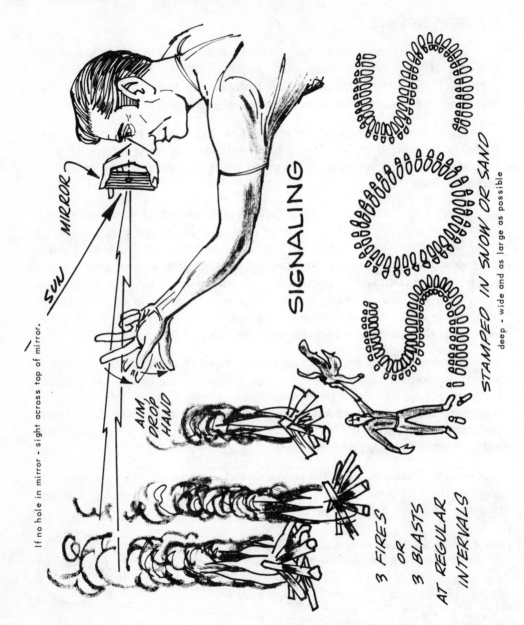

SIGNALING

If no hole in mirror - sight across top of mirror.

SUN

MIRROR

AIM DROP HAND

3 FIRES OR 3 BLASTS AT REGULAR INTERVALS

STAMPED IN SNOW OR SAND

deep - wide and as large as possible

6 ∘ ∘ BODY ENERGY

ENERGY INPUT, ENERGY OUTPUT — VERSUS TEMPERATURE

Foot travel in rugged environments is more strenuous and demands more energy than the average, everyday occupation. The outdoorsman must make provision for these energy needs in the light of possible environmental dangers, hostile weather, and distance from sources of supply. For it is energy replenishment, energy conservation, and protective body shelter that will sustain life during his travels.

In the quest for basic information for this brief chapter on energy sources and uses, our researchers asked one of our doctor members for some assistance. The doctor explains that in its need for energy, the human body is not unlike an automobile engine.

Most modern outdoorsmen know that an automobile engine in good condition can go so far on level ground on a full tank of fuel, in ideal weather conditions, at a constant speed. Any uphill, downhill, wind or rain, or change speed, will affect the distance the tank of fuel will move the vehicle before it stops from lack of fuel. If the vehicle is driven fast, the engine uses more fuel and the distance traveled is much shorter. If the vehicle is driven slowly and steadily, the distance is increased.

This same theory can be applied to the human body. So much body fuel — food, water and oxygen — will move the body so far under ideal weather conditions good physical conditioning, and at a constant pace controlled by calm emotions. Any uphill, downhill or fast walking will use more energy. Any change in weather can alter the rate of body heat loss and thus affect energy requirements.

Man, unfortunately, does not have a readable energy gauge that registers "Full — Half — Empty — Reserve" to help him determine the level of his available fuel. He depends on the physical signals of hunger and thirst — and habits he has acquired. During times of strenuous muscle action or emotional stress, these normal signals are overshadowed. It is then that knowledge and experience can prevent the outdoorsman from "running out of gas" at a critical moment.

Each person wherever he is, expends a certain amount of energy merely breathing, producing body heat, circulating the blood, and carrying on basic life processes. This basal metabolism uses about 1700 calories per day with the body at rest in an ideal 70° still air environment.

Foodstuffs produce the chemical energy necessary for these body functions, but the body can store only about a normal day's supply of energy in an immediately available or usable form.

The mechanism of food usage by the body is extremely complex and not completely understood in detail. All food, on digestion, contributes in some way to the metabolic pool. Certain specifics are extracted to build tissue; some of the fuel is used for immediate needs; some is converted to glycogen, a starch that is stored in the liver, and therein converted to glucose for quick energy. The remainder is processed into fat for long-term storage, or passed on as waste by the body.

The cell transforms this chemical energy into a variety of forms:

1.   The energy of the chemical bonds in the molecule of its own substance;   a chemical and osmotic energy.

2.   The mechanical energy of muscle contraction.

3.   The electrical energy of the nerve impulse.

During the transformation of this chemical and the contractions of muscles, heat is produced as a by-product. A by-product which helps to maintain the constant temperature needed for proper chemical transformation.

E.M.C. THE 3 ENERGIES OF LIFE

YOUR BODY HAS TRILLIONS
OF LIVING CELLS

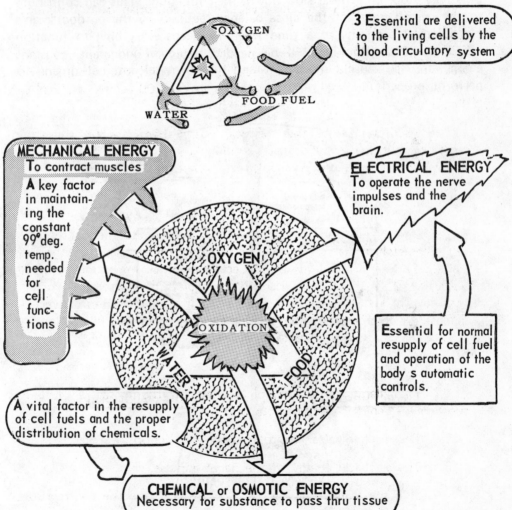

3 Essential are delivered to the living cells by the blood circulatory system

OXYGEN

FOOD FUEL

WATER

MECHANICAL ENERGY
To contract muscles

A key factor in maintaining the constant 99° deg. temp. needed for cell functions

ELECTRICAL ENERGY
To operate the nerve impulses and the brain.

Essential for normal resupply of cell fuel and operation of the body s automatic controls.

OXYGEN

OXIDATION

WATER

FOOD

A vital factor in the resupply of cell fuels and the proper distribution of chemicals.

CHEMICAL or OSMOTIC ENERGY
Necessary for substance to pass thru tissue

Of prime importance is the temperature of the body's inner core. Here the millions of tiny cells constantly recover the chemical energy liberated by the oxidation of foodstuff — a form of chemical energy that can work efficiently only in a constant temperature system of 99° F. A few degrees either way from 99° some of the millions of complex energy transforming cells may stop, or at least slow down, their functions. This can contribute to the overall upset of the close balance required by the outdoorsman's physiological economy at a time when he needs everything to function efficiently. Clear thinking will be needed for good judgment, constant energy for leg muscle movement and for the vital internal organs to perform properly.

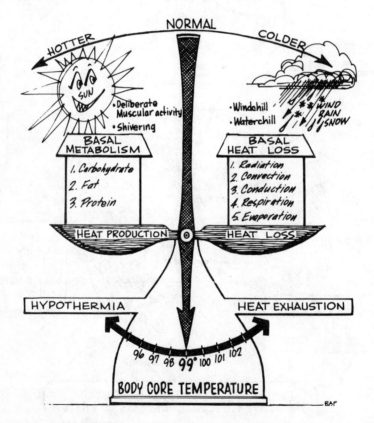

FACTORS AFFECTING THE BODY'S THERMAL EQUILIBRIUM

Life sustaining energy has much to do with how the body heat is maintained, because heat is released when muscles are moved — and muscles can be moved only when there is sufficient energy and will to move them.

Controlling this constant 99° temperature may well be the greatest problem of those who continually accelerate heat production by using muscle energy. The problems of temperature control by ventilation, removal and addition of clothing or changing pace are never ending if the outdoorsman is to complete his journey with adequate energy reserve, and his clothing free of perspiration wetness. Clothing wetness from perspiration, snow or rain is the greatest danger in cold and windy environments, while excessive body water loss is the greatest danger in hot, desert environments.

The constant body temperature of 99° is regulated by the sensory nervous system and the bloodstream. Sensory nerves convey information about the thermal state of the skin; the bloodstream about the state of the body as a whole. The heat regulating centers exercise control by means of nervous impulses, largely, but not exclusively, through the autonomic regulating system to cutaneous blood vessels, sweat glands and muscles. This means the flow of warm blood through the skin may be increased to promote heat loss (skin blush), or decreased to minimize heat loss (blue hands). The amount of water on the skin may be adjusted to provide the amount of evaporation cooling needed to maintain the constant heat balance. The activity of muscles may be regulated by relaxation in the heat, greater muscle tone under cool conditions, or increased shivering when heat production needs to be increased rapidly.

The outdoorsman will use considerably more energy fuel than the man working indoors, because of the energy lost to warm the cooler air he breathes and compensate for heat lost to cold, damp, windy elements. Roughly 10 percent of his energy production may be used just to combat extreme cold when the air is still. If the wind increases, energy expenditure increases drastically.

As for energy expenditure of the muscles in outdoor travel, hill climbing with a pack of supplies may use nearly four times as many kilocalories per hour as sitting at an office desk. It is not uncommon for an outdoorsman to expend 5000 to 6000 KC per day during a hike. Such expenditure of energy requires judicious planning and eating, as well as conservation of energy, if the outdoorsman is to return with sufficient energy to set up camp or drive home.

The effects of hot or cold environments upon the body are further discussed in later chapters. The brief discussion here is to show the relation of heat production by the cells to physiological problems of energy conservation in environments where exposure can deplete body heat faster than it can be produced, or raise the body temperature beyond that which can be tolerated by the human body.

DEHYDRATION AND BODY WATER NEEDS

The water requirements of the body are more serious than the food requirements. A person can live for a long time on the stored energy (fat), as long as he restricts energy output to the vital processes of life, with little or no physical movement. Even when living off his fat, man must have water or he will dehydrate; water and oxygen are required to convert fat into usable energy. This is a slow process. Body fat can be converted at a rate of only approximately two pounds of body fat every 24 hours. This slow conversion can sustain a person at rest for some time, as long as water is available.

The outdoorsman will lose body water by respiration, urination, and perspiration. Respiration and urination are understandably nearly constant; perspiration can be variable, and is controllable to some degree by the individual. Any amount of heavy work such as uphill hiking or travel in very hot environments will increase the body's sweat rate. The increase in heat production by muscle action causes the body's automatic regulating process to try to cool the body with perspiration.

Respiration will increase in proportion to the degree of heavy work, and result in an increase in water loss. Often the outdoorsman, in the excitement of his sport or the weariness of the rough terrain, will not drink enough water and dehydration will begin to reduce the blood supply volume and promote heat exhaustion. Further dehydration brings about disturbances of cell functions, which leads to muscular inefficiency, nervousness, depression, and possibly death.

Remember, it is the water in your body that saves your life — not the water in your canteen. Ration your sweat, not your water. Drinking water is the primary treatment for dehydration; desert experts advise a person to drink at least two quarts of water a day when at rest. If traveling afoot in an extremely hot environment, the body's requirements can leap to over one gallon a day. Drink all the water you need when you are thirsty and drink plenty of water with meals.

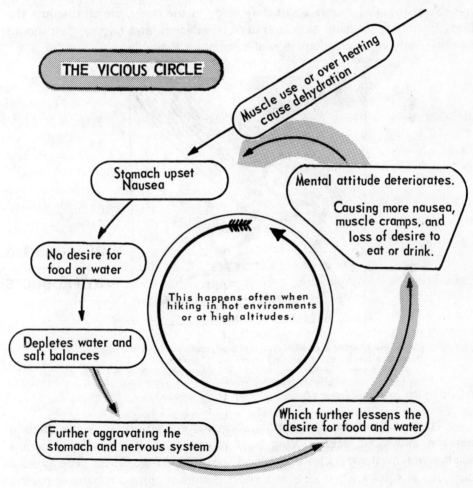

THE VICIOUS CIRCLE

Muscle use or over heating cause dehydration

Stomach upset Nausea

Mental attitude deteriorates.

Causing more nausea, muscle cramps, and loss of desire to eat or drink.

No desire for food or water

This happens often when hiking in hot environments or at high altitudes.

Depletes water and salt balances

Further aggravating the stomach and nervous system

Which further lessens the desire for food and water

DEHYDRATION DANGERS

Thirst discomfort is one indicator that your body needs water. A dark yellow color to the urine is the second and "danger" indicator. Other symptoms are slow motion, no appetite, nausea, drowsiness, and high temperature. When dehydration reaches 6% to 10% of the body weight, the symptoms will be dizziness, dry mouth, tingling in the arms, and inability to walk. Usually the problems of dehydration disappear rapidly with sufficient intake of water.

Sweating also causes a salt deficiency in the body, which disrupts the body chemistry, causing muscle cramps, headaches, and nausea. Salt should be taken only when an adequate water supply is available.

DETRIMENTAL

BY-PRODUCTS

Muscle use requires a continuous supply of fresh fuel from the blood stream.
Muscles in use burn the fuel and create waste products.
If the vital organs cannot eliminate these waste products from the veins fast enough the muscle may become saturated with CO_2 and Lactic acid.
This prevents delivery of any fresh fuel by the arteries.

The end products of food digestion and energy use are water, carbon dioxide, and lactic acid. During hard muscle work these waste products accumulate in the muscles and blood, resulting in weariness. Too great a build-up of these by-products in a short period of time can hamper muscle movement and hasten exhaustion.

The by-products that clog the system and disrupt its functions can be removed or flushed from the body only by rest, especially sleep. It is important to the outdoorsman to rest periodically during the trip to allow the by-products of energy use to be flushed from the muscles by the blood. A rest period of 15 minutes will remove approximately 50% of these wastes; a rest 15 minutes longer will remove only approximately 5% more wastes. This is the reason for a steady, comfortable pace, which allows the lungs to discharge the carbon dioxide, and allows the lactic acid and other waste products of energy use to be continually flushed from the muscles.

BODY CONDITIONING FOR OUTDOOR ACTIVITIES

Conditioning of the body has a direct effect on the way the body can assimilate the food fuels. Exercise actually improves the body's capacity for more exercise. Metabolism becomes more efficient, the blood moves more rapidly in carrying away the waste products from the muscles while re-supplying them with more fuel.

It is true that daily body conditioning during the weeks before strenuous outdoor travel will make the trip less tiring and more enjoyable. This should be accomplished with a well balanced diet, steady exercise and plenty of rest during the week before the trip.

During the period of strenuous activity, the physiological requirements of the body are energy and water. The most efficient diet during this time is sugar and water. Fats and proteins are usually contained in normal meals. But all meals before and during periods of hard muscular work should be small, easily digested, or followed by long rest periods. The reasoning for this is self-evident. The blood volume cannot serve two major users (lungs and stomach) at the same time. Attempting strenuous activity after a heavy meal usually causes stomach upset or muscle aches.

To be at his best in the morning, a sportsman would be wise to eat a good, balanced meal the night before and get eight hours of sleep. This should energize his body with a full supply of fuel, provided he has no illness or other complications, to start the day. A light, sugary breakfast of easily digested food will be converted to usable energy during the morning, and be available for use during the afternoon. Lunch should provide the energy needed to set up camp in the evening, with the body cleansed of accumulated muscle waste products during the night's rest.

If the sportsman has had a large, heavy breakfast before the strenuous exercise of uphill walking, chances are he will have to slow the pace so that the blood can serve both body functions, or suffer an upset stomach. As the day wears on, the sportsman will begin to feel better and claim he has his "second wind." In reality he has reached the point where all body functions have settled down to the routine of doing the tasks required. The blood flow and breathing have increased to provide the oxygen needed by the cells and muscles, body temperature is being controlled within tolerances, and metabolism has leveled off at a constant rate. "Second wind" is felt when the body processes speed up and are working smoothly, hence the man feels at his best.

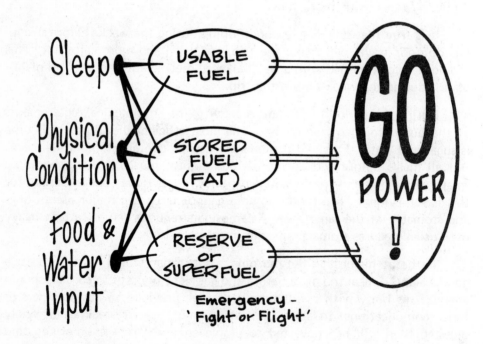

Preconditioning is the easiest way to enjoy outdoor activities that will demand strenuous activity. Or better yet, stay in good physical condition to feel better every day and live longer.

When we analyze the basic parts of the human body, we find that it is a rugged, amazing machine. It must be, because people put all sorts of odd foods and liquids into the stomach and it still manages to produce something useful to the energy pool. Even the structure that contains man's mass is rugged. Whenever you watch a skier cartwheeling down a slope you wonder how bones and muscle can take such punishment. Even though we batter, bruise and punch the skin full of holes, it still miraculously recovers, with time.

We know that you can abuse certain parts of the body without too great discomfort. But other parts are so delicate that they give up or stop functioning whenever the temperature of the body changes a few degrees either way.

Inside the body, every organ action has several interactions. Whenever one small part stops for any reason, it affects many other parts. The subtle interaction often compounds and sometimes obscures the original problem before it can be reversed.

To the outdoorsman facing hostile elements, the decisions relative to body shelter and energy expenditure are absolute. The right decision must be made or a situation may develop which compounds itself until, if not reversed, will end in complete physical collapse.

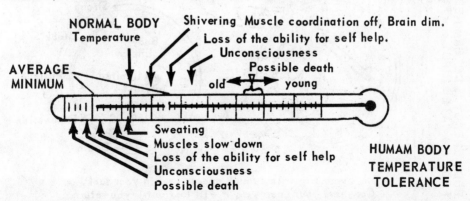

NORMAL BODY Temperature

Shivering Muscle coordination off, Brain dim.
Loss of the ability for self help.
Unconsciousness
Possible death
old ⟷ young

AVERAGE MINIMUM

Sweating
Muscles slow down
Loss of the ability for self help
Unconsciousness
Possible death

HUMAM BODY TEMPERATURE TOLERANCE

Often the right decision calls for waiting for more favorable travel conditions. This is not easy for modern people, who can't wait for anything. Today people are conditioned to instant relief from discomfort, boredom, hunger, and stress. This attitude, or way of life, creates a problem to someone trying to stay alive during a storm. The incessant wind, rain, snow, or cold not only causes discomfort but constitutes a severe mental stress. Worry about unfulfilled promises in town, delays, inconvenience to others, has to be suppressed. Often waiting is the only way to conserve energy enough to stay alive.

Energy is the outdoorsman's source of GO power, and becomes his most precious possession when away from civilization. It can be conserved to sustain life for a long time — or it can be exhausted in a very few hours. Energy can be used up by muscles or blown away by wind, depending upon the activity, state of mind, and type of body shelter.

Every outdoorsman has only a limited supply of usable energy. This amount is determined by his physical condition, amount of rest, amount and type of food input, amount and type of liquid input, recent expenditure of muscle energy, mental state, appropriateness of clothing for the environment, and the temperature and amount of wind and wetness.

Whatever remaining energy an outdoorsman has at a given time, the decision of how to use or lose it is his alone.

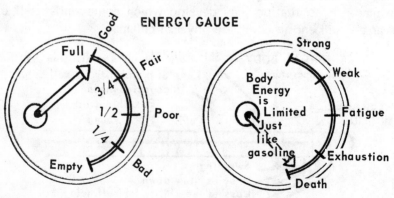

BODY ENERGY IS DETERMINED BY FOOD and WATER INPUT, and REST.

ENERGY GAUGE

Good · Full · Fair · 3/4 · 1/2 · Poor · 1/4 · Empty · Bad

Strong · Body Energy is Limited Just like gasoline · Weak · Fatigue · Exhaustion · Death

Start your trip with enough energy fuel in your tank.
Conserve your energy so it will last until you return.

WAYS TO CONSERVE HIKING ENERGY
IN MODERATE TEMPERATURES

Slow down — muscle use.

Stop sweating — Sweating is an indication of excessive heat production — and heat is a by-product of energy use. Sweating can precipitate dehydration.

Stay comfortable — Blue hands, numb fingers or any chilling is a warning of body heat loss. Keep wind from blowing away body heat. Add clothing insulation — keep cold from stealing body heat.

Stay dry — Clothing loses most of its insulation when wet. Wet clothes allow loss of body heat up to 240 times faster than dry clothing.

Stay calm — Fear, imagination, or blind determination may overrule good judgment. The uncontrolled mind allows panic reactions, causing waste of energy in useless or even detrimental activity.

Wear a hat — The brain receives 20% of the body's blood supply, and 25% of the oxygen intake. The unprotected head can radiate a large proportion of the body's heat.

Nibble foods — Eat small amounts of sugary food often as you travel.

Drink warmed liquids — Why waste calories heating cold water to 98.6°?

Rest — Don't travel till fatigued . Rest 5 to 10 minutes each hour to cleanse the blood of accumulated waste products.

CARELESS EV.   Says----

SLOW DOWN

CONSERVE ENERGY

DON'T SWEAT

STAY DRY

STAY COMFORTABLE

BEWARE OF------
              OVERHEATING
              WINDCHILL
              WETNESS

7.. SURVIVAL IN COLD

MAN IN THE COLD ENVIRONMENT

Man's survival anywhere in the world depends upon his knowledge of life's necessities and what can harm his body, his mind and his equipment. His ability to combat these enemies or improvise his necessities may be his greatest challenge.

Experienced outdoorsmen recognize that a man on foot in rugged terrain can be in or pass through desert type heat and Arctic type cold in the same day — or even at the same time. It is not uncommon for men to get frostbite and sunburn at the same time, or experience hypothermia (dangerous lowering of the body temperature). It just depends on the clothing worn (or not worn) and the weather elements prevalent in the area.

If the traveler is to be able to survive anywhere his feet can carry him, he should have knowledge of all the terrain and weather environments, under all the conditions, with all the stresses, that could or might prevail. But it would require volumes to cover all the variables of survival anywhere on earth.

When we analyze the real problem of man staying alive anywhere on earth, we find that man must first control the mind, for the mind controls all physical movement, as well as judgment. Loss of control may allow man's determination to drive him on and on to exhaustion of his limited body energy.

Second, it has been established that too much heat or too much cold have a detrimental effect on the mind and even on muscle movement, and can upset the delicate heat balance required within the body. So man should learn how to stay warm for survival in the cold, and how to stay cool for survival in the heat. With such knowledge man at least would be better able to cope with these insidious enemies.

Physical requirements for man's survival, basically, are simple. And if one is aware of the consequences of being without them, he may be able to improvise his needs from what surrounds him — such as providing protective body shelter.

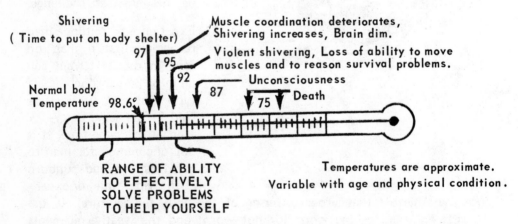

DANGERS OF A LOWERING BODY CORE TEMPERATURE

THE 3 SURVIVAL ENVIRONMENTS

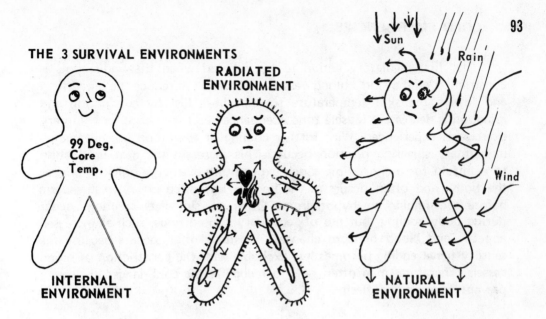

RADIATED
ENVIRONMENT

99 Deg.
Core
Temp.

INTERNAL
ENVIRONMENT

Sun

Rain

Wind

NATURAL
ENVIRONMENT

Cold and the Primary Physiological Responses:

Cold affects not just one or two specific tissues or functions of the exposed person, but affects the whole physiological economy in sometimes subtle, yet always complex, fashion.

Under cold conditions, humidity plays a minor role, unless the skin is artifically wetted (rain or perspiration). Should this occur, the resultant evaporation cooling may exceed all other factors in importance. A man immersed in sub-arctic 40° water can be cooled beyond recovery in about 20 to 40 minutes — or approximately 10 to 20 minutes in 33° water. A man in wet cotton clothing must consider he is nearly immersed in water, and act accordingly.

The interactive effects of air temperature and air movement are so inseparable under cold conditions that the term "windchill" is widely used to designate their combine effects.

As with heat, the regulatory process called into play to maintain the 99° heat balance in the cold environment represents a primary burden on the body and in turn sets up consequent disturbances that increase the total burden on the body.

The first regulatory action to be initiated when the body cools is constriction of the skin's blood vessels. This tends to reduce the blood flow and lowers the skin temperature so that heat loss by conduction and radiation is decreased. Muscle tone is enhanced and the desire for voluntary exercise is experienced. With further cooling of the blood the automatic, involuntary shivering reaction occurs. This increases the heat production to eightfold for a short time. Such expenditure of energy quickly fatigues the body, and often occurs as the body's last ditch effort to stay warm before succumbing to hypothermia. Other physiological reactions occur during body cooling, but are of secondary consequence, such as increased appetite and blood pressure changes. Frostbite often occurs because the sensory nerve ending becomes less excitable with the constriction of blood vessels. Therefore, man often fails to recognize the cold danger in time to prevent freezing the flesh.

Heat Production

Man's complex body heating system is based on his basal metabolic rate. This specific rate of heat production may be increased by diseases that produce a fever, certain body agents such as thyroxin or adrenalin, and by moving muscles.

During comfortable sleep, heat production drops to approximately 80% of the awake basal metabolic rate. However, outdoorsmen may have considerable problems in maintaining comfortable sleep because of inadequate equipment, insulation values, and the environmental stress.

Shivering, the body's automatic defense in combating heat loss, can produce heat equivalent to slow running. The ability to move muscles or to shiver will depend on the energy level in the body and the fatigue factors of the immediate past energy use. During strenuous hiking, heat production may increase from six to ten times the normal basal metabolic rate, creating problems of over-production. After six to eight hours of such work, a person's fatigue factors are high, energy level is low, and heat loss factors are increased by sweat-moistened clothing and slower muscle use.

Figure 1 shows the many factors that affect the thermal balance of the human body.

We all know the value of external heat sources — furnaces, fire, sunlight, etc. They become absolutely necessary to help support heat production during extreme cold. The fire and cups of hot liquids have a welcome warming effect. In fact, hot liquids have become standard first aid treatment for persons suffering from heat loss of hypothermia.

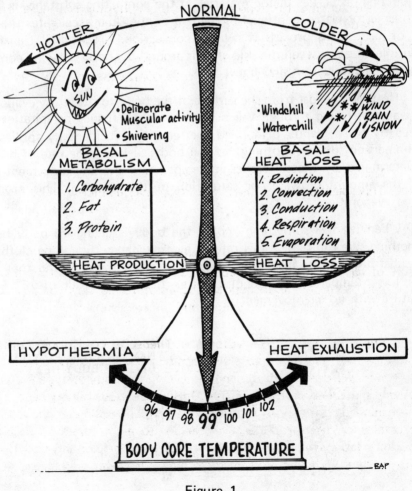

Figure 1

How Body Heat is Lost

Man feels the "cold" when body heat is being exchanged between man and his environment by any of these five physical processes: Evaporation, conduction, convection, radiation and respiration. Heat will be exchanged by conduction between the surface of the body and any material in contact with it which is at a different temperature. The speed of transfer is basically determined by the difference in temperature of the two and the heat conducting properties of the material. If the contacting substance is fluid — such as air or water, continual movement of the fluid accelerates the transfer of heat. This process is called "convection." Nearly all transfer of "sensible" heat between the skin and air around the body is by the combined process of conduction and convection.

Heat may be lost from the surface of the body to the air by evaporation of water diffusing through the skin from deep tissue (perspiration) produced by sweat glands, or applied (wet cloth) or accidentally applied (rain or immersion, or wet clothing) to the body surface. The rate of heat loss is determined by the difference in temperature and the movement of air and the amount of water or saturation of the clothing. This process is called evaporation.

When we feel something "cold" the body is giving up body heat to something. We can reduce this rate of heat exchange by adding clothing or by substituting some insulating material between the skin and that which has a lower temperature, or acquire shelter that encloses air of 75° F temperature with no air movement.

ANY TIME YOU TOUCH ANYTHING
LESS THAN 98.6 Deg. F . YOU
WILL GIVE UP BODY HEAT

Rock — Metal
Snow — Water

Heat Loss Dangers

Hypothermia means lowering of the body temperature within the body's core. Under the tongue, most people register 98.6° F on a thermometer. Since the body is such a complex mass, controlled by the brain and other automatic control centers, it will measure a different temperature at different locations of the body, because of the distance from the heart and the amount of flesh thickness and surface. The average human body has approximately 18 sq. ft. of skin surface. That is 18 sq. ft. of cooling and heat radiating surface. Flesh acts as an insulator for the deeper core areas of the body. Fat, being a good insulator, helps to prevent rapid cooling. Women, who have a thicker layer of subcutaneous fat, reputedly withstand cold better than men.

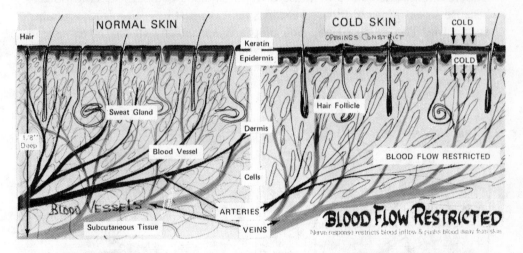

Since humans have so much skin, and it is the first part of the body to react to heat and cold, maybe we should take a better look at it. Skin approximately the size of the little fingernail and 1/8″ thick has 100 nerve endings, approximately 3 feet of blood vessels, and many sweat glands, which will react to protect the core from hypothermia or hyperthermia. These make your skin one of the more complex of the body regulators. The nerves respond to heat and cold with amazing rapidity to defend the body's temperature. Also, the central automatic defenses will sacrifice hand, arms, feet and legs to defend the inner core from cold. That is why you can suffer frostbite and frozen hands and feet yet still be walking and talking.

The skin and the micro environment next to it are the inner core's major protectors. Animals use fur to protect this vital temperature zone. They instinctively seek shelter during adverse weather. Outdoorsmen, determined to reach a predetermined goal, travel amid nature in the same weather conditions animals seek shelter from. Since few outdoorsmen have a fur skin, they use layers of clothing to regulate this micro environment. The traveler on foot away from modern technology and the comforts of artificial heat, must be constantly alert and ready to protect the body's micro environment from heat loss.

The man pictured in Figure 2 is losing heat five ways. Many times you have used these same heat loss principles to cool yourself on a hot day. Understanding the values of these different means of heat loss is important because in extreme cold these heat loss factors must be recognized as dangerous to life. Too much of any one of the five could mean death from hypothermia. If you know and recognize what is stealing body heat, you may be able to solve the problem and improvise the necessary defense against the loss.

Man's thermo-regulatory system is designed with a greater heat eliminating capacity than heat conserving capacity. This is partially explained by the fact that the threat of hyperthermia is a more serious problem than hypothermia. It ultimately is easier to carry and add more body clothing to protect from heat loss than to carry a refrigerator to cool the body. Either condition can incapacitate the unpreapred, uneducated person very quickly in temperature extremes.

The Five Mechanisms of Body Heat Loss

RADIATION is a major cause of heat loss in most situations. The body is like a large radiator 70% full of hot water. Just like a home radiator, it heats the body's micro environment.

Your head, being the most important part of the body, receives the most blood, oxygen, and hence the most heat. It has been stated by doctors that heat loss is so rapid from an unprotected head that 50% of the body's total heat production may be lost at 40° F temperature, and up to 75% of the total body heat production when the temperature is 5° F. Covering the head will conserve body heat and energy. This may be why the old mountaineers always say, "When your feet are cold, put on your hat." Experienced outdoorsmen wear parkas with attached hoods to get maximum protection from wind and rain.

RESPIRATION: In cold environments, the air we breath enters cold and leaves warm. This accounts for a significant amount of heat loss. Naturally we cannot stop breathing to prevent this heat loss. But we can pre-warm the air we breath by installing a wool scarf across the face.

CONDUCTION heat loss becomes noticeable whenever the skin touches anything less than body temperature. In artifically controlled environments, such as a home (about 70°), this heat loss is minor. But sweaty or rain-wet clothing touching flesh can extract heat at an alarming rate.

Mountaineering doctors warn outdoorsmen to watch the temperature not of the air, but of the wet clothing touching the skin.

Outdoorsmen have many problems of heat loss by conduction. They carry metal sporting equipment, wear special metal gear, such as crampons, handle cold metal objects, and sit and sleep on snow, ice, and wet ground. Besides traveling in cold, wet and windy environments, they normally use more muscle energy, often overproducing body heat. This can create a major problem of sweat-wet clothing, causing body heat loss.

EVAPORATION is the natural way the body cools itself. Sweat glands in the skin excrete water whenever the body temperature is above normal. This body water may then be evaporated to the air, causing heat loss. The amount of evaporation of heat loss on a given day is determined by the relative humidity of the surrounding air.

To the outdoorsman who over-produces heat, sweating is a never-ending problem of ventilating and regulating clothing. An Idaho mountain man's maxim is, "To stay warm and alive in severe cold, don't sweat." Experience has proven this maxim correct. Clothing must ventilate or breath to allow water vapors to pass. If not, ice may form on the inside of the clothing.

Sweat saturated clothing, or rain wet clothing, cause rapid chilling of the skin. They must be removed in cold environments to prevent a combined conduction-evaporation heat loss. "Don't sweat" is the only way to conserve energy and prevent wetting of vital clothing.

CONVECTION of warm air away from the body surface is a primary method of heat loss. The body continuously warms the thin layer of air (micro environment) next to the skin by radiation. This micro environment is close to body temperature and is regulated by the clothing we wear. The dead air spaces between the layers of clothing are the barriers that prevent a rapid transfer while in still air.

The horizontal motion of air, causing transfer of heat, is accurately termed advection. The process of washing away the warm body air by moving air creates a wind chill factor that can exchange the micro environment's air faster than the body can warm it. The wind chill effect is basically due to this washing process: convection of warm air away from the body, replacing it with cooler air. For still air cold conditions we need, thick layers of dead air spaces, such as provided by down or other fluff-filled clothing. In wind, the quality of the clothing fabric and the size of the inter-spaces between the weave determines the amount of warm air transferred. Large knit wool sweaters are fine in still air, but allow fast transfer when the wind blows.

Wind Chill:

Without any wind, the body (normally covered) can withstand a greater degree of cold. But let the wind blow, or even a slight breeze, and the heat loss and energy loss become critical.

Figure 2   illustrates a wind chill chart used by Environmental Services personnel. The combined effect of wind and temperature is expressed as an equivalent temperature which is the effective temperature acting on exposed flesh. For example, we start a hike when the temperature is 50 degrees Fahrenheit and the air is moving at 10 miles per hour. The chart shows that the chill effect on exposed flesh is a cool 40°. But as we near a high point on our hike, the wind has picked up to 30 miles per hour and the temperature has dropped to 40°, giving us a very cold 13° on exposed flesh.

WIND - CHILL CHART

ACTUAL THERMOMETER READING °F.

Estimated Wind Speed MPH ↓	50	40	30	20	10	0	-10	-20	-30	-40	-50
	EQUIVALENT TEMPERATURE °F.										
Calm	50	40	30	20	10	0	-10	-20	-30	-40	-50
5	48	37	27	16	6	-5	-15	-26	-36	-47	-57
10	40	28	16	4	-9	-21	-33	-46	-58	-70	-83
15	36	22	9	-5	-18	-36	-45	-58	-72	-85	-99
20	32	18	4	-10	-25	-39	-53	-67	-82	-96	-110
25	30	16	0	-15	-29	-44	-59	-74	-88	-104	-118
30	28	13	-2	-18	-33	-48	-63	-79	-94	-109	-125
35	27	11	-4	-20	-35	-49	-67	-83	-98	-113	-129
40	26	10	-6	-21	-37	-53	-69	-85	-100	-116	-132

Wind speeds greater than 40MPH have little additional effect

| LITTLE DANGER FOR PROPERLY CLOTHED PERSON | INCREASING DANGER | GREAT DANGER |

DANGER FROM FREEZING OF EXPOSED FLESH

Figure 2

To use the chart, find the estimated or actual wind speed in the left-hand column and the actual temperature in degrees F. in the top row. The equivalent temperature is found where these two intersect. For example, with a wind speed of 10 mph and a temperature of -10° F, the equivalent temperature is -33° F. This lies within the zone of increasing danger of frostbite, and protective measures should be taken. It is emphasized that the wind-chill chart is of value in predicting frostbite only to exposed flesh. Outdoorsmen can easily be caught out in 30° temperature. Winds of 30 mph will produce an equivalent wind-chill temperature of -2 ° or below zero.

Water Chill:

The thermal conductivity of water is 240 times as great as that of still air, primarily because the greater density of water means more molecules of cold matter are touching the skin. To the outdoorsman, this means that wet clothing could extract heat from your body nearly 200 times faster than dry clothing.

When clothing gets wet, it loses 90% of its insulation value, so it no longer provides a layer of warm air next to the skin. Instead it clings. Wet clothing conducts body heat through the fabric to the outside cooler air. Sweat or rain-saturated clothing must be considered dangerous because it may cause heat loss conditions as severe as a dunking in the river.

Men who must work in cold, rainy, windy environments swear that wool clothing helps to keep them warm. This is because wool does not wick water like cotton. Wool and some synthetic fabrics do not absorb water into the fibers and actually dry faster. Whatever the reasons, rescue statistics have proven that victims dressed in wet wool generally survive over those dressed in wet cotton. (Obviously, staying dry, in either fabric, would be better yet.) Several worthwhile experiments may be found under "Improvising Experiments" in this book.

Many doctors and researchers have explored the causes for fatalities from exposure to wet, windy and cold conditions. Their conclusions are that energy and heat loss to the environment could be prevented by:

1.   Recognizing the problem before it becomes critical.

2.   Avoiding fatigue or exhaustion. Avoid sweating.

3.   Preventing excessive heat and energy loss with the better insulation of dry clothing and windproofing.

4.   Rewarming to normal those who are shivering before further travel.

The prevention of hypothermia rests entirely with the outdoorsman who, while traveling away from civilization may encounter unexpected weather, which can kill. Since few persons can be prepared for all emergencies, physically, mentally, or materially, they must make the best of what they have with them. If dressed in cotton, beware of getting wet. If not adequately clothed or sheltered, retreat and go another day. Staying dry is the only way to stay warm. Conserve your limited energy.

The essentials to prepare for and to prevent hypothermia are:

1. Know the Enemies — Cold, Wind, Wetness. Recognize their insidious power. Recognize your personal strength and the strength of those with you.

2. Prepare in advance for the worst weather. Carry or wear complete body protection. Use it before you get chilled.

3. Plan to refuel the body. To combat cold you must move muscles to produce heat. Sugary foods, nibble foods, are quickly converted to energy. Plan to carry extra food.

4. Always carry a plastic emergency shelter. A tube tent or large leaf bag can shelter the body from wind and rain. Such emergency gear is not much larger than a handkerchief and can be a lifesaver on a wet, windy ridge when you are storm-bound.

5. Make camp early in a storm. Cold has such a deteriorating effect on the body you must make camp while you have the energy reserves to pick the best possible site. Remember, the exhausted persons caught in extreme weather may perish before a shelter can be constructed of natural materials. Shelter construction takes time, energy, and visibility.

6. Keep moving. Since body heat is produced by moving muscles, it is essential that you manage some movement during the cold emergency. Avoid violent motions. You may cause more heat loss through your clothing as well as more energy loss. The best exercise is isometric muscle contraction. Prevent "pump action" ventilation.

Hypothermia has varying degrees of severity. The following rectal temperatures are approximate and variable, according to age, physical condition.

HYPOTHERMIA

Inevitably, if heat loss continues, the temperature of the body's inner core will begin to fall below 99 degrees. As the core (rectal) temperature drops, symptoms are as follows:

99 to 96 degrees: Shivering becomes intense and uncontrollable. Ability to perform complex tasks is impaired.

95 to 91 degrees: Violent shivering persists. Difficulty in speaking,

90 to 86 degrees: Shivering decreases and is replaced by strong muscular rigidity. Muscle coordination is affected, producing erratic or jerky movements. Thinking is less clear; general comprehension of the situation is dulled, and may be accompanied by total amnesia. The victim is generally still able to maintain posture and the appearance of psychological contact with his surroundings.

85 to 81 degrees: Victim becomes irrational, loses contact with environment and drifts into stupor. Muscular rigidity continues. Pulse and respiration are slowed.

80 to 78 degrees: Unconsciousness. Victim does not respond to spoken word. Most reflexes cease to function at this temperature level. Heartbeat becomes erratic.

Below 78 degrees: Failure of cardiac and respiratory control centers in the brain. Cardiac fibrillation. Probable edema and hemorrhage in lungs. Death.

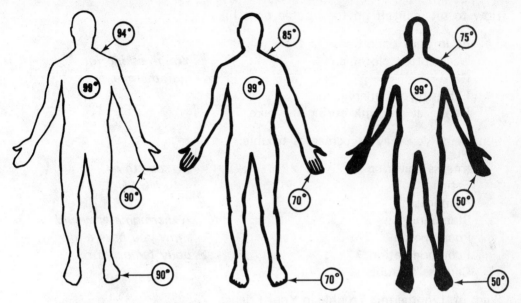

Treatment for the victim of Accidental Hypothermia:

Prevent any further heat loss any way possible.
Replace wet clothing immediately.
Shelter from wind and weather.
Insulate from ground conduction heat loss.
Force exercise, if possible.
Administer hot (110°) drinks.
Furnish an external heat source
   (fire, hot rocks, canteens, or
   other bodies).

Hot liquids — quickly!
(Only if victim is
conscious.)
Flesh-to-flesh contact
if no other heat source
available.
Work fast — the victim
is in real trouble.

In advanced hypothermia the body has lost the internal power to rewarm itself and it must be rewarmed — from the inside out, if possible, as with hot drinks. Fast heating from external sources drives cold blood into the core. Use caution.

How to set yourself up for trouble on a hike:

Be in poor condition.
Wear cotton clothing.   *You're asking for*
Get wet.   *hypothermia.*
Exhaust your energy.
Don't eat or drink during the hike.

Symptoms you may recognize as trouble:

Intense shivering   *Do something*
Fatigue   *NOW!!*
Numbness
Stumbling   *A thermometer would*
Poor Speech   *show you have a low*
Poor orientation   *body temperature.*
Careless attitude

Signs of Hypothermia Trouble in Your Friends:

Poor coordination   *STOP!*
Slowing of pace   *Take care of the victim*
Stumbling   *immediately.*
Forgetfulness
Hallucinations   *15 minutes from now he*
Thickness of speech   *will not be walking*
Dilation of pupils   *unless you rewarm him.*
Decreased attention
Careless attitude

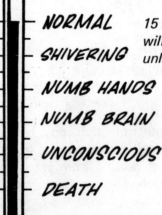

NORMAL

SHIVERING

NUMB HANDS

NUMB BRAIN

UNCONSCIOUS

DEATH

Effect of Clothing in Cold Environments

Clothing is only a protective shelter that we carry around. The immediate effect of adding clothing to the nude body is to trap a certain thickness of virtually dead, body-warmed air from the cooler air that was formerly circulating past. The effectiveness of the clothing will depend upon the rate at which heat passes across the space between the skin and the clothing barrier and through this barrier.

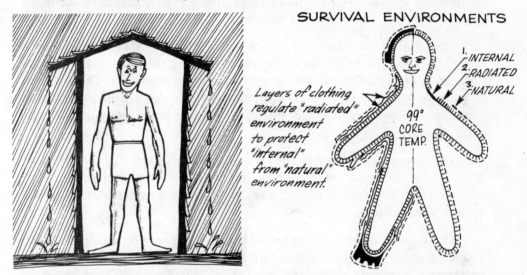

SURVIVAL ENVIRONMENTS

Layers of clothing regulate "radiated" environment to protect "internal" from "natural" environment.

1. INTERNAL
2. RADIATED
3. NATURAL

99° CORE TEMP.

Transfer across the space between skin and clothing depends upon the distance between them and on the rate of air movement within the space. Where clothing touches the skin, as when clothing is pressed against the body by contact with the colder ground or solid objects, by wind or by the hang of the clothing, the transfer of heat will be rapid. And where wet clothing touches the skin, the resultant conduction and evaporation heat loss will be rapid — often at the same rate as immersion heat loss.

Transfer of heat through clothing, itself, may take place in several ways: Through conduction through the fibers, such as metallic fibers in the clothing, nails in shoes, buttons, etc.; through conduction or convection, radiation, evaporation, or through the dead air held in the interstices between the fibers of the weave. If water replaces a large part of the interstices, then the heat conductivity of the fabric is greatly increased. Such wetness greatly increases heat loss by evaporation and conduction. This can become the outdoorsman's greatest problem in stormy weather.

The radiation absorption effect of clothing can be a great help in cold environments. Dark clothing absorbs radiant heat from the sun and reflective clothing repels heat. The openings of clothing — neck, arm and leg cuffs, zipper openings, all contribute to heat loss to some degree, and often allow the greatest amount of heat loss due to the pumping action of warm air next to the skin during body movement.

Cold that affects the body can be minor or severe. The backyard wind that chills the skin and numbs the fingers is just a reminder that the body surfaces need better protection or a change of environment. The cold felt by a person out in a wet, windy winter snowstorm can set up physiological reactions in the body that can be fatal in a few hours without adequate body protection.

The severe cold of the Arctic or the wind and blizzard of the Plains are prone to freeze unprotected flesh in minutes. Even the animals with hair and fur coats struggle to live through wind and sleet storms accompanied by low temperatures.

The type of fabric and the cut of the clothing have much to do with its insulation value, freedom of movement, constriction of blood flow, warm air transfer, water retention, and ventilation of excess body heat generated by muscle action during outdoor exercise.

To the outdoorsman dependent upon the clothes he wears and carries to keep his body warm, dry and sheltered during his travels, the choice of clothing should have the highest priority. Because of weight limitations, weather factors, seasonal conditions and the environment, his clothing must serve many purposes, yet be strong enough to withstand the abuse of the rough, rugged environment.

Several layers of easy-on-easy off, lightweight clothing offer layers of dead air for insulation between the fabrics. Wool fabric is preferable, as it is a non-absorbing fabric and has the unique property of keeping the body warm even when it is wet. However, the loose weave of the woolen fabric leaves much to be desired in a windstorm. So a wind stopper is advisable as an outer garment to minimize loss of the body-warmed air that is trapped in the large air sacs of the weave.

Cotton fabric has excellent properties in warm or moderate climates, and even provides excellent layer system dead air spaces for insulation against cold, as long as it remains dry. The danger of cotton fabric is that it absorbs and retains water, making it a deadly combination when it gets wet from rain, snow or perspiration. Cotton is very slow to dry because of the complete saturation of the fibers. Cotton clothing can become so saturated with water that the body heat loss can be nearly as great as when the body is totally immersed in water. Very wet cotton can lose heat nearly 240 times faster than dry cotton clothing.

To the man who continually produces excess heat by nearly constant burning of energy to move muscles, perspiration wetness is a perplexing problem that requires alert and constant attention to ventilation. Often the outdoorsman has to slow his pace considerably just to prevent wetness of underclothes. In extreme cold, windy conditions, he must quickly substitute dry clothing or warm shelter once the muscle activity is halted, or experience chilling and excessive body heat loss. Anywhere, any time, clothing/shelter is what allows man to live in harmony with the environment.

Since few outdoorsmen manufacture their own clothing, they have to purchase the best type of fabric and design possible within the limits of their pocketbooks.

Ever since buckskins and spinning wheels went out of style, man has been relying upon someone else to manufacture his outdoor clothing. Most of the clothing worn for comfort in the artificial environments of the city was not designed to protect the body when away from a controlled-heat shelter. In fact, much of the clothing sold by merchants for general use has not been designed for any weather at all. The criteria for clothing today are determined by fashion, fad, cut, color and economics.

Wool clothing still remains the best all-purpose outdoor clothing. Regardless of the itchy-scratchy problem, the majority of experienced outdoorsmen and outdoor workers, such as loggers, roadbuilders and construction men, wear them. Possibly these men have field tested these alongside of other workers wearing other fabrics, who were cold, wet and miserable.

The choice is yours. Many fabrics are available, many styles, many weights and lofts. What protects the body today in fair weather may be a millstone in tomorrow's storm.

Whatever type of clothing you are wearing when you get wet, remember it is the cold water held in and around the individual fibers that is holding the water next to the skin. Wring excess water out of the clothing. Fan it in the air. Whip it against a tree or rock. Put it back on only if you do not have dry clothing immediately available. Wet clothing is worse than no clothing under certain conditions — air temperature, wind, and sunlight are the variables.

We all know that damp, wet clothing may be dried by wearing it — but it will be at the expense of energy (heat) loss. The problem of wearing wet clothing is yours alone. Only you can feel the coldness, only you can calculate the time/weather/distance factors against the misery/energy/dangers.

Things to look for in outer weather garments:

Fit: Loose — large enough to add clothing underneath.
                Easy off, easy on (buttons vs zippers or Velcro
                Freedom of movement for arms, legs, and shoulders.
                    (Sleeves should be long for warmth).
                Wrist bands should not restrict blood flow.

Workmanship: Hood permanently attached.
                Pockets covered.
                Type of zipper and buttons — You will be trying to
                    use these with cold fingers.

Ventilation: Be sure you can open and close ventilation openings
                    easily. This is very important to help control your
                    body's micro-environment.

Fabric: Weave, density, and loft.
                 Water absorbency or repellency of fibers
                 Drying and matting problems
                 Strength and quality
                 Color — important for signaling or camouflage.
                 Insulation value of filler material

The clothing you wear may be all you have when the storm approaches. Analyze its effectiveness, then act judiciously to protect the body.

Improvising Outdoor Shelters

Shelter is only clothing at a distance. It may or may not include artificial heat producers, such as stoves. A shelter may be constructed of any material (lumber, bark, paper, cardboard, plastic, snow or dirt) and utilize insulation materials (snow, dirt, paper, fabric, bark, wood, cardboard, air) to help reduce body heat loss by convection, evaporation, radiation or conduction.

In emergency situations, such as wind and rain storms, where shelter is mandatory, man would be wise to do what the local animals do — burrow in, or crawl under foilage. In forested areas it is faster to burrow or hollow out a small shelter under a downed tree than to find suitable material to erect a shelter. Time spent constructing such a shelter can be costly in energy and body heat loss due to more exposure to the very conditions that the shelter is to protect from. Fire light and warmth are a comfort, but not if you must be further exposed to hostile elements. Attempting to build a fire in rain may be futile — it not only is nearly impossible but you just get wetter gathering fuel. Seek shelter and stay dry.

Shelters are as varied as man's imagination. They differ with every situation, depending upon the immediate danger, natural or man-made materials available, time allotted, energy use limitations, and the type of body protection needed.

A shelter must serve the immediate needs of the builder. Each shelter should be built to provide a minimum of body heat loss and a maximum of body protection.

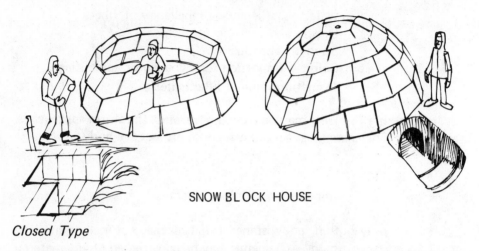

SNOW BLOCK HOUSE

Closed Type

Closed type or small area shelters sealed against the wind, rain and cold are necessary in cold environments where the body heat is used as the primary heat source. These shelters can provide a minimum of cold air transfer with the outside cold air. All closed type shelters should be small and have all holes plugged with snow, bark, dirt or boughs, unless a gas stove or open flame is used in the shelter, which requires a high and low vent to remove carbon monoxide.

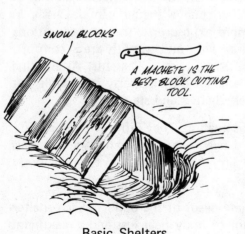

SNOW BLOCKS

A MACHETE IS THE BEST BLOCK CUTTING TOOL.

0° OUTSIDE

SNOW DRIFT

VENT

32° INSIDE

PLANNED OR IMPROVISED INSULATION

3 HOURS BUILDING TIME WITH BEST TOOL — A SNOW SHOVEL

Basic Shelters

In a forested area, burrow in under a log; use bark and boughs as siding material and ground insulation. This is by far the quickest and least energy-consuming technique.

In areas devoid of forest, dig snow caves or snow trenches, or build rockeries to gain the desired protection. Snow caves take hours to build and require some type of tool, such as a shovel, mess kit or hard hat, for removing the snow. Snow is a good insulator. Caves dug into deep snow banks are quite satisfactory. Keep your clothing dry when digging. Work slowly to avoid excessive sweating. Perspiration-wet underclothes should be changed or removed and used as outer clothing once they are wet.

A snow cave in 6" deep powder snow necessitates special construction and requires about three hours to complete. First select two 6 ft. sticks. Drive one vertically into the ground and use the other to draw a 12 ft. circle around this stake. When finished, place the stick on the ground with one end touching the stake. Shovel the fluffy snow into the circle, packing it down until it is approximately 1 ft. above the vertical stick. Let the snowpile set for about an hour, then tunnel into the pile following the guide stick. Remove snow to the warmer ground and make a small room with two-foot thick walls. Remove vertical stake.

POWDER SNOW SHELTER

SHELTER DITCH IN MINIMUM SNOW DEPTH OR POWDER SNOW

SOIL OR DUFF

TRENCH SHELTER

In wooded country make a tree pit shelter, if snow is deep enough. Enlarge the natural pit around a large tree trunk and roof it with any readily available covering — ice blocks, limbs, canvas. Use boughs and bark for insulation.

Camp in timber, if possible, to be near fuel. If you can't find timber, choose any spot protected from wind and drifting snow. Don't camp at the base of slopes or cliffs where snow may drift or come down in avalanches.

Try to keep the openings of all shelters closed to the wind or construct a wind break.

Metal aircraft or automobiles will become as cold as the coldest air temperature. If unable to improvise a small nest within the vehicle from available insulation on walls, rug, ceiling, seats, paper, maps, etc., consider another type of improvised and insulated shelter — away from the super-cold metal.

Generally, the auto or aircraft will provide the most desirable shelter, except in extremely low temperatures.

Open Side Shelter

In forested areas, where you have an ample supply of boughs, bark and limbs, a simple bough-roofed shelter will give some protection from rain, wind and snow. Construction takes time and energy and offers only

a minimum of body protection. A fire and heat reflector can help to warm the shelter and dry clothing.

Mountain Rescue personnel advocate the simple, under-the-log shelter illustrated in the drawing above.

Find a log with a hole under it. Hollow it out. Use slabs of bark to enclose your nest. Plug all holes. Keep living area small.

Cold Weather Clothing:

Proper clothing, correctly worn, is important in keeping warm and dry. Wool clothing is the best to wear in wet or cold conditions because it does not absorb water. The large air sacs give good dead air spaces, which trap and hold body heat. Insulation is largely determined by the amount of dead air space enclosed in the garment.

At night, arrange dry spare clothing loosely around your shoulders and kidney region. When you are cold, breathe through a loose weave cloth or face mask. Breath moisture will freeze in below-freezing temperatures and seal a tight fitting mask, so be sure the scarf, sweater or face mask is always loose. Cold air is warmed by the body to approximately 98° at the expense of energy. Prolonged exposure is harmful to lung tissue.

Moisture from any source is deadly during cold extremes. Sweat is moisture that wets the inner clothing. Prevent sweat by slowing down your activities to below the sweat level or ventilate by removing outer clothing until comfortable. Keep removed clothing handy to put on when you stop the heat-producing activity.

Keep head, neck and ears covered to prevent excessive heat loss. Watch out for tight clothing and tight boot laces. It is the air space between the layers that keeps you warm. Mittens are better than gloves when necessary to flex fingers for warmth. Flex toes often to prevent frostbite. In very cold conditions this may be necessary every step.

When exposed to wind use everything and anything feasible to stop the wind from blowing away your body heat. Wear tarps, plastic bags, rain gear or wind proof clothing with maps, paper, or cardboard.

If you fall into water in a cold environment, hasten into dry clothing. If this is not possible, roll in dry snow to blot up moisture. Roll, then brush off snow; roll again and again until all water has been absorbed by the snow. Do not take off shoes untill you are in shelter. Change to dry clothing as soon as possible. Cold will be intense once you are wet, and in a few minutes you will be incapable of removing your clothing without a buddy's assistance. Never travel alone.   If your feet are cold wiggle your toes constantly.

In very low temperatures, wet clothing can be dried by freezing and then beating the ice crystals out of the fabric.

Prevention of getting wet is far better than clever techniques of re-drying. Avoid all open water. Don't cross a snow-covered lake unless you are sure there is firm ice under the snow sufficient to support your weight. Stay dry — it is the way to stay alive in the cold.

Hazards of Cold Environments.

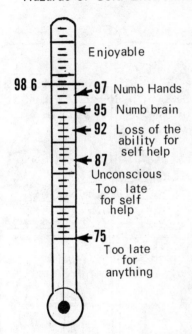

Cold is miserable unless you have planned and prepared for it with adequate body protection. The effect of cold on an unmittened hand is numbness of fingers, with loss of dexterity. This numbness slowly climbs from fingers and knuckles to wrists, with varying degrees of pain.

Cold, once it cools the insulating layer of skin and starts to lower the inner core temperature of the body, or trunk, below 95° will continue lowering at an ever-increasing rate. Unconsciousness often occurs as quickly as several hours.

In cold, rainy, windy conditions, all persons must be alert for the symptoms of accidental hypothermia (lowering of the body temperature) in themselves and in fellow travelers.

Watch for:

1. Recurring stumbling and poor control of arms and legs.

2. Dazed, care-less attitude, with decreased attention span.

3. Uncontrolled shivering — drowsy — confused.

4. Weak, unable to maintain muscle movement.

5. Collapse — Serious emergency — requires immediate treatment.

Treatment of a conscious victim of hypothermia: Remove his wet clothing. Dry the skin off. Reclothe him in dry garments or put him in a sleeping bag with another person, unclothed, to transfer warmth by contact. Build fires or place heaters around the victim. Caution must be used not to burn the skin when using canteens of hot water, heated rocks, etc., as a heat source.

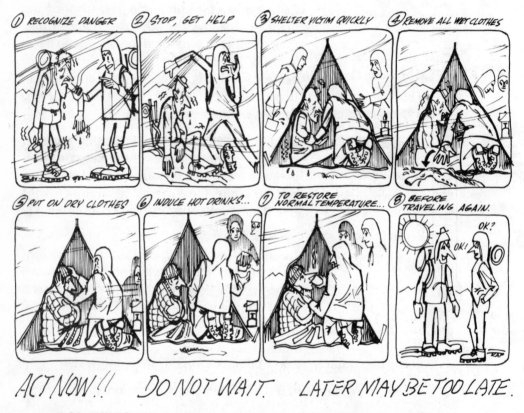

ACT NOW!! DO NOT WAIT. LATER MAY BE TOO LATE.

HYPOTHERMIA will threaten your outdoor activity. Expect it to happen.
Be alert, because it is impossible to self-diagnose after gaining a foothold.

Give him lots of hot, sugary drinks. Do not attempt to travel until the victim is fully aware of what is going on around him. (Test temperature by gulping liquid yourself)

Treatment of the unconscious person is very touchy, and should be done in a hospital, if possible. Rewarming too fast can cause fibrilation of the heart. The best treatment is to dry him, reclothing in dry garments; place the person in a warm tent and let him breathe warm air, with body-to-body contact for slow rewarming. If immediate evacuation is available — put victim in sleeping bag and rush to hospital for rewarming and treatment.

For all persons, a cold emergency is a critical situation which requires constant alertness to prevent frostbite, freezing and body temperature loss.

Cold affects not only man, but may also alter the operating condition of mechanical vehicles and other equipment that may be the only source of travel. All metal, chemicals, plastic, and lubricants react to intense cold. Consideration must be given to possible failure of equipment.

All metal and non-freezing fuels can become as cold as the lowest temperature of the surrounding air. Spilling gasoline or antifreeze on bare skin can cause severe frostbite. Touching super-cold metal without gloves or insulation causes nearly instant freezing. Do not pull free unless you want to lose some skin. Thaw loose. Use warm water or urinate.

Caution and deliberation must be exercised in everything done in extremely low temperature. Man's thinking, physical competence and dexterity are decreased. Move slowly. Avoid sweating. Never travel without a buddy. You watch him and have him watch you. Cold slows both mind and body — "a numb brain is a dumb brain."

In cold, wintery conditions, protection from the cold is your immediate and constant problem. Check for frostbite, avoid snow blindness, keep dry. To stay dry, keep snow off clothing, out of boots and gloves. Avoid all open water. Over-exertion causes perspiration, which will collect inside clothing, decreasing its insulating value and increasing the chance of frostbite.

Do **not** attempt to travel without mittens, head cover and overboots. These can be improvised from any fabric — they do not have to be sewn and perfectly fitted. They are to protect the extremities from the cold. Your whole body must be kept warm to maintain circulation to hands and feet. Excessive loss of heat from any part of the body restricts circulation, leaving the extremities with little heat, thus susceptible to frostbite. Stay dry.

If over-snow travel is absolutely necessary in soft snow, improvise snowshoes from boughs, metal, or anything that will support your weight on top of the snow.

Frostbite: Should you accidentally incur frostbite, you will recognize it by the grayish or yellow-white spots on the skin. Warm the frozen part rapidly on bare flesh under armpits or stomach. If hot water is available for the thawing procedure, use nothing hotter than 105°. Do not rub frozen flesh or forcibly remove gloves or shoes. Once frozen flesh is thawed, do not allow it to refreeze.

Freezing:

The old wives' tale of freezing to death if you go to sleep is true — **if you allow the air to carry away heat faster than your body can produce it.** Prevent excessive heat loss any way possible.

You can sleep or doze safely in cold areas with little danger of freezing, providing you are in good physical condition and have ample energy reserve. Your brain will awaken you when the body cools to a point that it needs exercise to create body heat. Then it is safe to doze again. Do not attempt this without a good reserve of energy.

Snowblindness is caused by exposure of the unprotected eye to the glare on snow. This can occur even on cloudy days. Prevention is the best care. Wear dark glasses or improvise glare shades by cutting small eye slits in any material suitable to tie around the head. Treatment of snowblindness is cold compresses, aspirin, and wearing a lightproof bandage. Victim will generally recover in 18-20 hours but must use caution to prevent recurrence.

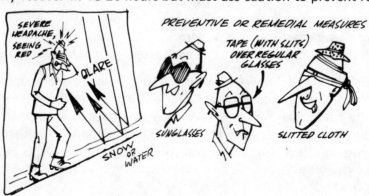

SEVERE HEADACHE, SEEING RED

GLARE

SNOW OR WATER

PREVENTIVE OR REMEDIAL MEASURES

TAPE (WITH SLITS) OVER REGULAR GLASSES

SUNGLASSES

SLITTED CLOTH

Sunburn: Sunburn can occur in snow country. Cover up in bright sunlight. Use approved sun creams. Reflected sunlight can burn inside nostrils, under chin and in ears. Don't compound an emergency with more problems — cover up and prevent sunburn.

Carbon Monoxide Poisoning:

This is a great danger in cold areas where gasoline stoves must be used inside tents, snow caves, etc. This deadly gas is odorless and colorless. Prevention is easy: maintain good ventilation whenever a gas stove, heater or lamp is burning. Never go to sleep when one is burning. Turn it off.

If your gas stove burns with a yellow flame, it is not getting enough oxygen and is creating carbon monoxide. Lift the pot off the stove often to check the flame. If it's yellow, ventilate! If blue, relax.

Since carbon monoxide is heavier than air, it will effect first those persons who are lying on the ground. And if they are asleep in a sleeping bag, you may not notice they are being affected.

Usually there are no symptoms of this poisoning, because it very subtly attacks the oxygen carrying capacity of the blood circulatory system. You may feel burning eyes, dizziness, throbbing temple pressure, sharp headache, or pounding pulse. Get out immediately. Breathe deeply. In others — look for blue lips, drowsiness, muscle twitching — get them into fresh air and, if necessary, apply mouth to mouth resuscitation immediately.

Water: Dehydration is almost as great a problem in cold conditions as on the desert, because all the water is frozen into snow or ice. Some streams or lakes may provide access to water (use extreme caution against falling into the water). If the sun is shining, you can melt snow on a dark plastic or tarp, flat rock or any surface that will absorb the sun's heat. If you melt snow by heating over a stove or fire, put in a little snow at a time and compress it — or the pot will burn. Agitating, as with a stick or knife, will speed up the melt time. If water is available, put a little in the bottom of the pot and add snow gradually. If ice is available, use it. You get more water for the volume with less heat and time.

If fuel is plentiful, try to drink at least two quarts of hot beverages or water daily, instead of cold water. Water taken internally will be heated to 99° at the expense of energy loss.

Travel in Cold Environments

If the decision to travel has been reached, after consideration of the requirements of food, fuel and shelter, and destination, equip yourself as best you can. Don't travel in whiteouts, blizzards or bitter cold winds. Make camp and save your strength until better weather. Never travel with poor visibility. Use available equipment or improvise over-snow needs. Carry or sled all of your clothing, sleeping bags, food and fuel.

STAYING ALIVE IN A COLD EMERGENCY

First Stage

Get out of rain — wind — storm.

Make body shelter — Improvise quickest adequate type for terrain and conditions.

Analyze the approximate length of the emergency and chances of assistance.

Analyze personal dangers:
Severity of body heat loss.
Local environmental hazards.
Amount of remaining energy.

Analyze resources:
Adequate clothing — insulation.
Emergency equipment — shelter — warmth — fire — signals.
Transportation.

Add body insulation — loose fitting wool clothing in layers.
Shelter the head and neck from wind and cold.
Close all clothing openings.

Put on windproof and rainproof clothing to reduce heat loss.

Improvise artificial heat — fire — stoves, etc.

Stay put in shelter until conditions improve. Conserve energy.

Do not travel if visibility is obscured.

Second Stage

Don't get wet. Wet clothing loses body heat 240 times faster than dry clothing.

Don't sweat. Indicates excessive energy loss and gets clothing wet from inside.

Stay calm: Worry causes imagination to blossom; imagination causes poor judgment.

Conserve energy — Don't travel in a storm.
>The remaining energy is all you have to produce life-saving body heat.

Stay comfortable — Add clothing insulation as needed.
>Loose fitting clothing in layers creates dead air space insulation.
>Shelter head and neck. Close all clothing openings.
>Put on windproof and rainproof clothing to minimize wetness and body heat loss.

Nibble Food and Drink:
>Get artificial heat — fire, if possible. Drink hot drinks.
>Nibble on food — to resupply energy.
>If food is not available, conserve what energy you have.

Stay put — Don't fight a storm.
>If visibility is obscured, don't travel. Shelter is the primary need.
>Most storms are of short duration.

Tips:
>Pre-warm inhaled air by breathing through a wool cloth or scarf.
>Sit and stand on thick insulation, wiggle toes and fingers.
>Keep stored water from freezing.
>Stay dry. Don't sweat.

If skin is numb, watch for frostbite.

When traveling or working, watch for signs of stumbling, poor reflexes, care-less attitude. They indicate exhaustion — and exhaustion can be 30 minutes from death.

Watch for equipment damage by cold. Protect fuel and water supply.

Improvise mittens, overboots, and body insulation.
Pioneers have survived a severe storm wearing bark from trees.

The clothing you wear may be all you have when the storm approaches. Analyze its effectiveness, then act judiciously to protect the body.

For clothing to effectively keep you warm in cold environments, remember this word — COLD:

Clean dirt-clogged air interspaces do not trap insulating dead air.

Color: Black absorbs heat, white reflects it.

Overheating:
Ventilate. Avoid overheating. Perspiration wets fabrics the same as rain.

Layer System:
Easy on, easy off layers to help regulate body temperature.

Dry: Keep all fabrics dry. Wet clothing loses 90% of its insulation value.

SURVIVAL IN HEAT

MAN IN THE HOT ENVIRONMENT

Radiation of heat from the sun has changed nearly one-fifth of the world into arid, desert-like areas, where the heat is so intense that little grows or lives. What little rain does fall to earth in these areas is quickly evaporated, runs off, or sinks deep, leaving the surface inhospitable to man, beast, or vegetation.

The term desert has many connotations. To some it is all sand; to others it's a rock, salt or gravel wasteland. Deserts come in all shapes and can be rugged landscapes, rough, gullied or mountainous. Whatever the terrain, it is a place that often has extremes of temperature every day, from very cold at night to very, very hot during the sunlight hours. At times some of these areas can be beautiful and full of color. Then again, they can become a roaring wind or sandstorm which tears at everything in its path.

Millions of people have learned how to live in hot environments. They know they must respect the heat and the power of the sun. They know the dangers, and they adjust their lives to meet its daily challenge.

A stranger to this land can adapt. He can live in harmony with heat if he is aware of the dangers and knows the physiological responses to heat that will take place in his body and knows how to prevent their destructive onslaught.

Regardless of where man is, hot environments have a detrimental effect on his mind, his body, and his equipment. This does not necessarily have to occur on a desert. It can be in a valley of still air, where the temperature rises because of the lack of air movement; or on the reflected snow on the south face of a mountain. Even the reflected heat of concrete streets and buildings of the big cities can cause a localized very hot environment. Too much heat in any form can quickly upset the delicate balance of man's inner core temperature and even cause death.

Effects of Heat on the Human Body

The chemical and physical processes that constitute life are very susceptible to the effect of temperature. If the temperature of the tissue in which they operate changes by only a couple of degrees, they tend to get out of balance. As with cold, the regulatory processes called into play to maintain heat balance can set up consequential disturbances which often compound the problem.

The first corrective action is for the heart to pump more blood to the blood vessels out near the surface of the skin. Here the sensory nerves dilate the blood vessels and let the too-warm blood circulate close to the skin's cooler surface. This cools the blood by radiation, conduction and convection — but only as long as the air temperature is cooler than body temperature.

This first stage of body heat reduction is continuous as long as the inner core temperature remains high. When part of the blood fluid is set aside by extreme dilation of the skin blood vessels, and the blood is not being pushed back to the heart, it will threaten the volume-capacity ratio

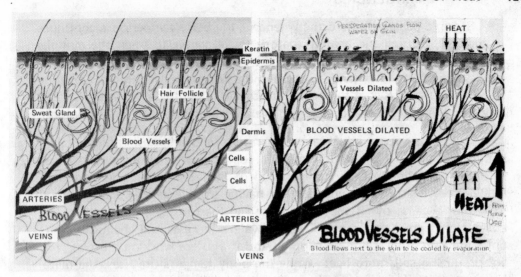

NORMAL SKIN   WARM SKIN

of the body's closed circulatory system. The heart may beat faster, but if the blood is not returning in sufficient quantity, it cannot function properly. This one physiological reaction, if prolonged, can upset the whole body and threaten the most vital organs.

Dilation of the surface blood vessels also increases the leakage of fluids from the capillary blood vessels, causing more blood volume loss from a supply that is already inadequate. This imbalance of volume-capacity ratio in the blood circulatory system appears to be the prime cause of heat exhaustion.

Whenever the inner body temperature rises above 99°, the heat regulatory system calls for insensible or sensible perspiration to cool the skin with water. Insensible perspiration occurs automatically when a minor temperature rise triggers the heat regulatory center. It is called insensible because it is water diffusing through the skin and evaporating before it becomes visible.

Sensible perspiration occurs whenever the body temperature continues to increase, causing the heat regulatory nerve center to open the millions of tiny sweat glands which perforate the skin. The sweat glands can secrete large amounts of water (and heat) upon the skin to be evaporated. Sweating alone, does little to cool the body, unless the humidity is low enough to assure that the water is evaporated. High relative humidity retards evaporation.

If you experience a high air temperature (above 90°) and high relative humidity (above 75%), your body will be doing everything possible just to hold the optimum body temperature of 99°. This cannot go on indefinitely. Your heart is pumping fast and having trouble getting enough blood to pump, because of all the blood stored in the surface blood vessels. The sweat glands are pouring perspiration (water) and essential chemicals (salt) onto the skin from a limited supply. And if you are working muscles, you are producing still more heat. While the body temperature rises, the metabolic rate, itself, is increased; waste products increase, and the nervous system is disturbed.

THE DOUBLE PROBLEM

INNER and OUTER HEAT PRODUCTION

MUSCLE HEAT PRODUCTION

IN A HOT ENVIRONMENT

INCREASES THE TOTAL

HEAT PROBLEM FAST

Watch for it and slow down your heat production before it stops you permanently.

To be able to live where extremely high temperatures can be expected, one must first recognize just how serious the local heat problem is and plan to adjust his activity to lessen the load of heat production and absorption. Then plan and prepare to do everything possible to keep the body temperature from rising further.

Environmental heat affects everyone differently and the severity increases with age. The degree of heat that would cause heat cramps in a 16-year-old may cause heat exhaustion in a person of 40 and heat stroke in those over 60. Generally, the real thermal problem has to do with the reduction or collapse of the body's ability to dissipate heat by circulatory changes and sweating, or a chemical (salt) imbalance caused from too much sweating. This allows the inner core temperature to rise to critical levels.

Knowing the basic effect of heat, one should prepare to counteract its action before it becomes destructive. It can disable the stranger to heat in less than two hours.

Water Requirements of the Human Body

Water in the body and on the body provides the most effective coolant to control the inner body temperature. But it also may be the most limited coolant available to the outdoorsman in a desert situation. Water is the third requirement of life — exceeded only by air and body shelter. The human body is approximately 75% water. Intake and output of liquids are necessary to the processes of life and the normal functions of the vital organs. When water loss exceeds intake, dehydration takes place.

Humans lose water three ways: perspiration, respiration and urination. The first two are the automatic processes that remove excess body heat from the body. Urination removes the waste products of food oxidation and muscle or energy use. There is little a man can do about these automatic water losses, but it is useful to know their insidious effects. Losing water to the extent of 2½% of body weight, or approximately 1½ quarts of body water, will reduce his efficiency 25%. If he is working, walking or playing in a temperature of 110° F, his normal ability will be reduced another 25%. The sweat rate of one hiking in hot conditions can increase to two quarts per hour.

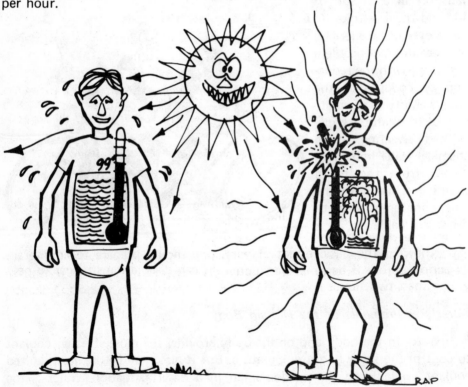

BODY WATER IS LIMITED
Excessive perspiration can limit your life.

Reduced ability quickly becomes a critical factor in desert emergencies, where water and salt resupply are limited. Dehydration symptoms are shown in a very subtle way. Often you do not feel these symptoms because of their gradual attack upon the total body. Water loss and the accompanying electrolyte deficit affects the entire body; the body's automatic controls will follow Nature's rules in determining the most urgent need for water at the moment, and will draw its needs from the water stored in the tissues and then the blood. Since the human body is approximately 75% water that is stored and used in so many of the processes of life, it is hard to determine which function will be affected first by dehydration. The first stages of dehydration are so similar to a host of other problems that even the medical men sometimes overlook them. Loss of appetite, drowsiness, nausea, lack of desire to move muscles, general discomfort, are the first warnings of a water deficiency.

Secondary warnings of dehydration are a bit more noticable: headache, dizziness, dry mouth and yellow urine. And if that doesn't tell you that you need water, the fact that your legs are rubbery and you can't talk right should scare you into drinking water or conserving the little you have left.

Third stage warning symptoms are so drastic that you may see it in others (too late for self diagnosis). The victim is down and having spasms and talking strange. Tongue may be swollen, senses diminished. Treat with water, salt and shade.

To an outdoorsman, his first warning of serious dehydration is the color of his urine. A dark yellow indicates that his body is short of water. Thirst is easily suppressed, and a person desperately in need of water physiologically need not feel unduly thirsty. For this reason, all survival manuals urge that you drink your water as you feel thirsty. Do not hoard water. For further explanation of dehydration and salt deficiency, reread the chapter on Physiological Problem Indicators.

Calcium deficiency contributes to fatigue and muscle cramps by increasing your susceptibility to lactic acid build-up and bone breakage. Calcium intake should be increased before strenuous outdoor activities.

Tables in Figures 4 & 5 on page 132 condensed from
Arizona Civil Defense booklet.

The optimum ways to conserve body water are to lessen the heat load — slow down activity. Rest in shade, hike in shade of canyon walls — keep clothing on. Keep mouth shut. Get up off the hot ground (it can be 30° cooler a foot above the ground).

In any hot environment, drinking plenty of water and replenishing salt losses are the requirements for staying physically healthy. But in the desert your life depends on your water supply. Figure 4 shows how long you can survive on specific amounts of water with a maximum temperature of 110° F in the shade. Figure 4 and 5 typify approximate travel and life expectancy.

TYPICAL WATER NEEDS IN THE DESERT	
If You Sit Quietly	
If you have this much water	You will probably die after
No water	3 days
1 gallon	4 days
2½ gallons	5 days
5 gallons	7 days

Figure 4

Never enter the desert without a map. Desert maps show water holes.

If you walk each night until exhausted and sit each day in the shade —		
If you have this much water	Travel this far	You will probably last this long
No water	10 - 15 miles	2 days
1 gallon	20 - 30 miles	3 days
2½ gallons	30 miles plus	3½ days

Figure 5

Heat That Kills the Unprepared

Outdoorsmen who travel into hot environments, such as deserts or arid areas, have to plan for the worst. Being aware of the problems is not enough — one has to be prepared to provide water, shade and body protection, and all of life's necessities. Most hot, arid regions do not have water or ready shade.

Radiated Heat: The sun can make metal, rocks and sand 30° hotter than the air — hot enough to fry eggs on. And if it can fry eggs, it can burn flesh. Just walking or lying on hot ground or among hot rocks causes the body to gain heat. Touching any metal can burn the hands.

The sun's ultra violet radiation can burn exposed skin (even tanned skin) and the burn will retard sweating. So remain completely covered with lightweight clothing that reflects heat and sunlight. Wear a head and neck shade. Don't fry the brain — it's your best survival tool, and your life will depend upon sound decisions now.

In some areas a man can last only a few hours in the direct sun. If you have shade shelter, stay there. If you don't have shade, make some.

IMPROVISED SHADE

Shading the head, and especially the back of the neck, appears to be extremely critical because of the close proximity to that part of the brain which contains a vital nerve center for the control of breathing and circulation. The sides of the neck have several high volume arteries close to the surface, which supply 20% of the body's entire blood flow to the brain. If the neck's skin surface is absorbing abnormal quantities of radiant heat, this may heat the blood and the brain to the critical level and possibly cause sun stroke or heat stroke.

Don't travel during the very high heat of the day. Your problem is keeping the body temperature from rising above 99°, which is not easy when the ground around you is 125°. Wait till the sun is lower on the horizon. Waiting is hard to do when you know loved ones are worrying. But waiting in the shade is the only way to survive long enough to return to them. Waiting a few hours can often make a difficult task easier and safer, or allow the storm to pass.

Heat can cause such a drastic upset of the physiological processes within the body that a person just hasn't the desire to do much of anything. Although anxiety about the situation can override this, and persons have been known to die while digging their stuck car out of the sand. Lost persons have pushed on and on till they dropped from the heat.

What to Do to Beat the Heat

You know the blood volume-blood capacity will be threatened by loss of blood volume due to dilation of skin blood vessels. You know that the heart is having a serious problem getting enough blood to pump. You can help by slowing down muscle activity and cooling the body any way you can: Shade, fanning, wetting the skin. Lessen the demand on the heart. If you are perspiring this gives you a clue that you are dehydrating, or losing water and salt, both of which are necessary for the body to function. Dangers of dehydration are shown in Figure 3.

If you have water, drink it whenever you are thirsty. Conserve what water you have in your body. Keep lightweight clothes on. Clothes retain the sweat and reduce loss by evaporation. Take salt in small amounts, but only as long as you have water to drink with it. You may feel more comfortable without clothing on in the heat, because your sweat evaporates faster. But you will lose more water — and without body covering, sunburn of bare skin can compound your problem.

Desert areas are the most common, but not the only places, for an outdoorsman to find too much heat. Heat which could challenge his ability to stay alive long enough for assistance to arrive or for him to improvise his life-sustaining needs.

The increase in body temperature can occur in many ways. For instance, a person hiking uphill in heavy clothing can perspire enough water and salt from his body to cause dehydration and heat cramps — and if he is in the direct sun with little air movement, this can develop into heat exhaustion or heat stroke very quickly. The first symptoms are so vague that people often disregard heat problems in favor of other problems, such as fatigue, out-of-condition, heavy load, indigestion, headache, nervous tension, etc. People on salt-free diets or those who have failed to drink enough water in the deep canyons of the big cities, can experience heat problems, ignoring the first symptoms or mistaking them for indigestion or nervous tension or hangover.

Heat cramps often impair hikers who forget to replenish salt lost by sweating on a steep trail. Heat cramps are caused by loss of salts from blood and tissue due to excessive sweating. These painful muscle cramps may respond to firm, hard pressure and relaxation, but respond best to resupply of the salt loss. Salt and water management is your personal responsibility.

Acclimatization to Heat

Conditioning for hot environments is as beneficial as conditioning for a fair weather hike. This allows the body to adjust to meet the greater demands for salt and water. Acclimatizing gives the body time to adjust the perspiration rate and chemical actions within the body. Accustom yourself to an adjusted pace — slow down and increase your work efficiency. The most important aspect of acclimatization is adjusting the body to tolerate more heat while decreasing heat production.

Activities in the Heat

When the temperature rises, most people slow down. Lack of desire for muscle activity is probably caused by the disturbances in the blood flow, and it could be an automatic process to lessen the chance of more heat load due to muscle heat production. Whatever the reason for slowing down activities, it helps to cool the body.

Water, metal, buildings, concrete, snow, rocks, salt flats, white sand, anything which will reflect sunlight or retain heat from direct sunlight, can cause local hot spots. Be wary of such areas, or prepare in advance for intense heat.

A person should not attempt any activity that will cause more heat production or body temperature increase. If a person absolutely must work, he should work a few minutes then rest in the shade. Time spent in construction of shade for the work area would be well spent. If perspiring heavily, drink water. Cool the body any way possible.

Play or enjoyment ceases whenever the inner body becomes too warm by only a few degrees or when the water and salt supply becomes low. If the conditions persist and are not reversed, enjoyment not only disappears but a person quickly becomes helpless and unable to take preventive or corrective action.

Hazards to Health During Heat Emergencies

Sunburn: Exposure to the direct sun is always dangerous — it can cause burns that are painful or even fatal. Sunburn is caused by overexposure to ultra violet radiation. Treat by cooling the skin, applying approved burn medications, and avoiding further exposure.

Sunblindness: Caused by direct or reflected sunlight. Symptoms are burning, watery or inflamed eyes, headaches, and poor vision. The best treatment is prevention, but once sunblinded, protect the eyes from all light and relieve pain. Wear a lightproof bandage and bathe the eyes frequently with cold, wet compresses. Generally the victim will recover in 18 to 20 hours sufficiently to travel with dark glasses.

Exposure to extremely high temperature, high humidity, and direct sunlight may cause four types of heat problems: Heat weakness, heat cramps heat exhaustion, and heat stroke or sun stroke.

Heat weakness: Generally caused by excessively hot, humid environment. Symptoms are easy fatigue, headache, mental and physical inefficiency, poor appetite, insomnia, heavy sweating, high pulse rate, and general physical weakness or loss of strength. Treatment is to drink plenty of water, get to cooler environment, replenish salt loss.

Heat cramps: Usually are caused by strenuous activity in high heat and high humidity, where heavy sweating depletes salt level in the blood and tissues. Symptoms are cramps in the legs and abdominal wall or painful spasms of voluntary muscles. Pupils of the eyes dilate with each spasm. There may be heavy sweating; skin becomes cold and clammy. Unlike stomach aches or abdominal disease symptoms, heat cramps are intermittent.

Treatment: Keep the patient resting; give him salt dissolved in water — but only if plenty of water is available. Often water alone will precipitate the problem; salt deficiency is the primary cause.

Heat exhaustion: Usually is caused by physical exertion during prolonged exposure to heat, which precipitates the overall breakdown of the heat regulatory system and disrupts the circulatory system, causing insufficient supply of blood.

Symptoms: A person is first weak and may have heat cramps, while sweating heavily. His skin is moist and cool, with inner body temperature near normal. The face will be flushed, then pale, with pulse thready and blood pressure low. He may vomit or become delirious.

Treatment: Place the person in the shade, flat on his back. Give him salt with plenty of water. Since he is cold, keep him wrapped up and even give him hot drinks, if available. Severe cases may be very serious. If no response to first aid, seek medical help immediately.

Heat Stroke and Sun Stroke: These are caused by a failure of the heat regulatory system which causes the automatic process of body cooling by sweating to stop. This is serious because when the automatic cooling stops, the inner body temperature can quickly rise to over 106°. Heat stroke is brought on by excessive sweating under conditions of high heat, high humidity, radiation absorption, or muscle activity in a windless environment, where the thermoregulatory system is being overworked. Advanced age or illness can be contributing factors.

Symptoms: Weakness, nausea, headache, heat cramps and even mild heat exhaustion. Body temperature will rise rapidly, pulse will be pounding, and blood pressure is high. Delirium or coma is common. Sweating will stop just before heat stroke becomes apparent. Armpits will be dry. Skin is first flushed and pink, then turning to ashen or purple in later stages.

Treatment: This is a serious medical emergency. Move to a cooler environment and cool the body any way possible. Get medical assistance fast. The internal automatic heat regulatory system is out of balance and has stopped functioning. Body temperature must be regulated artificially from outside the body until the heat regulatory system can be rebalanced.

Any of these hazards to health can occur anywhere and any time the environmental temperature and humidity increase simultaneously. The problem may occur anywhere or any time a person can become overheated by physical exercise or sweat profusely.

Emergencies in Hot Environments

Most emergencies will be only of one or two days' duration, and travelers can live through them provided they try to help themselves and do the right things first.

Stay out of direct sun. Improvise body protection (shade).

Slow down all body heat production

Signal your distress: Colored flags — clothing — panels — smoke — mirrors. Do everything possible to make yourself more conspicuous and easier to be seen.

Conserve your body's water: Don't sweat — and retain the sweat in light clothing. Try not to urinate. Drink water when thirsty. Don't die with water in your canteen.

Foods like proteins increase metabolic heat production and increase water loss. When faced with a short term heat emergency, food is not necessary for life, but water is. So don't eat. It will only make you thirsty and dry you out.

Don't fight the elements. Stay put under shelter. If caught afoot in a sandstorm, stop traveling. Mark your direction of travel with anything available, then lie down with your back to the wind and rest. Cover the face with a cloth. It may be uncomfortable, but it's the only way to stay alive.

Digging a vehicle out of the sand during the hot part of the day in direct sunlight may be your last effort. Resting in the shade and delaying the project until later in the day, when it is cooler may allow you to get home alive.

However, modern people who are strangers to hot, barren, uncivilized environments, often take a dim view of waiting even a short time in this forsaken place and sometimes their imagination is filled with visions of dried bones. Fears can overpower good judgment, replacing it with a determination to escape. Desert rescue teams say that many fatalities are caused by people attempting to walk back from a short outing into the desert, where their vehicle has become stuck in the sand or has developed mechanical problems.

Almost any vehicle can get you so far away from civilization in a few minutes that you cannot walk back alive.

Whenever the sunshine is direct or reflected, expect problems. Whenever the ground is powder dry and devoid of greenery, expect heat problems. Whenever the area has no moving air or wind, expect the heat to rise quickly.

Desert Shelter Requirements

Body shelter from the direct sun will be the most urgent requirement during the heat of the day. Keep clothing on, cover the neck, and get out of metal vehicles. Improvise shade on the breezy side of the vehicle with a tarp or brush. Try to sit a foot above the ground; it will be 30° cooler. Use caution when leaving car doors open. Often this turns on interior lights, which drains the battery of starting ability, leaving the vehicle useless as a means of getting you back to civilization.

If traveling on foot in canyons, try to travel in the breezy or shaded side, when possible. Rest in the shade of bushes and available trees.

IMPROVISE SHADE ---
or PERISH ! ! !
the choice is yours alone

Clothing or body shelter is necessary to retain water and to prevent sunburn. A light-colored hat and neck shade is a must to protect the temperature of the vital brain area. Better to wear a bush hat than none at all.

The desert often is very cold at night, so never discard clothing. Sometimes in an emergency a person can dig down to yesterday's sun-warmed sand to keep warm during the cold nights. It doesn't hurt to put sand over you like a blanket. Some desert areas have such temperature extremes that the body heat loss becomes the prime danger during the night hours.

Desert Travel Hazards

Heat and unfamiliar environments tend to magnify the hazards. Desert emergencies are seldom planned, and therefore have a disturbing effect on the individual and his ability and will to live. Regarding travel, all desert survivees advise: if you don't know exactly where you are, stay put.

Do not try to walk cross country or take a shortcut. Most American desert or arid areas are criscrossed with thousands of trails, roads, dry washes and animal tracks. Some of these have long been abandoned. In fact, many vehicle drivers report being lost for hours on a maze of roads that seemingly go nowhere. If you find a well used road going in the right direction (use compass to be sure) stay on it. Shortcuts can compound your problem. Mirages or heat waves often mislead the novice with false visions, but generally are recognized as such before causing difficulty.

Travel on the desert is rough on feet and on energy consumption. Soft sand makes slow, tiresome walking. Deep dust is nearly as bad. Cross country travel generally consists of crossing dry washes or up and down shallow canyons. Travel in deep canyons is not advised if you are lost, because search planes have a hard time spotting you. Energy-consuming routes should be avoided.

Desert people advise anyone walking to stay on any blazed trail or man-made   road or railroad which shows recent signs of being used. Check the direction of travel with a compass to be sure. Use your map or make one of where you have been. It is surprising how often lost persons get unlost when they sit and think about where they have been.

If the weather is raining or thunderheads persist, be wary of the dry washes, which can quickly become raging torrents of water. Rain usually makes roads impassable and foot travel slippery, all of which bolsters the rule of staying put when lost on the desert.

If you are walking, your feet suddenly become your third most critical point — right after energy and water requirements. Feet will swell from insensible perspiration and heat; and if boots are removed they may be impossible to get back on.

Do not travel when you cannot see where you are going. Storms have many ways to hide your guiding landmarks. Travel in darkness over rough terrain usually adds more injuries and more problems to those you already have.

Sandstorms and dust storms are not pleasant experiences. The stress on the nervous system is almost unbearable. Lie down with your back to the wind. Cover your face with a cloth and wait out the storm.

Finding Water in Desert or Arid Areas

There are a few general rules for finding water in desert and arid areas and in the foothills. The best is a good map which will show established water holes. All efforts to find water by searching and digging underground will consume energy and water, and increase water requirements. Hence a person should analyze his emergency situation and water requirements very carefully, weighing all probabilities of being reported overdue and searched for. If he can expect to be missed and can expect the search will start within 12 to 24 hours after he was due back, it may be wiser to sit and conserve what body water he has.

Many desert areas are patrolled by aircraft. If near flyways, your distress signals may be seen and reported. For example, if you planned a two-day trip into the desert and were expected back at a specific time, chances are you will be found in three days, provided you remain with your easily seen vehicle and help yourself to be found with various distress signals. If you are afoot and not near your vehicle, expect the worst. It may take days and days for searchers to find you, so plan to fend for yourself.

Water generally is found wherever there are signs of vegetation. The greener the vegetation or the taller the trees, the better the chance of finding water. Generally the bottom of a canyon or the base of a hill is the most likely. Small springs or seeps will support green growth on the shoulder of a mesa. Often these springs or seeps disappear in a short distance.

Digging for water is not always profitable. Some green vegetation has long roots (20 to 30 ft.) that reach deep for water. Dig only a few feet down in the best possible location. If no encouraging signs of damp sand, look in a different spot. Dry stream beds often have water just below the surface. Try digging at the lowest point on the outside of a bend in the stream channel.

Dew sometimes forms on metal auto hoods and airplane wings, or on plant leaves that can be sponged with a cloth. Some water can be obtained as dewdrops on the under side of a plastic sheet spread on the ground during the night. Use every possible means of water conservation and supplementing your water supply.

Some plants have capabilities for water storage, but efforts to get sufficient water from these plants is often unsuccessful. The best source of water in hot, arid environments is the solar water still. This ingenious device, when properly set up and lined with vegetation, can produce a pint of water in about three hours. Since it is slow, set it up early in your rest period during hot hours.

Insulate stone weight. It can be hot enough to melt the plastic.

Clear plastic - best. Translucent colored plastic - fair. Opaque plastic - very poor.

Dig hole 2' deep and 3' wide. Fill with any plant material. Don't puncture the plastic!

Figure 6 — Desert Solar Water Still

It takes approximately 3 hours for this still to start operating or to restart after opening.

Set it up in the morning, and it will work while you rest in your shade shelter.

Waterless areas occur even in moderate temperatures. Many trails on the beaches or in the mountains go for miles without crossing a stream. Even these dry up during certain seasons of the year. Beaches, however, offer easy water for the one who is equipped to dig for it. Dig a well farther away from the salt water. Strain it or wait for the mud to settle.

Poison springs are fictional, but be cautious of drinking from a spring or water hole with little green growth around its edge or little evidence of animal use. A small taste test is always advisable. Some water has high mineral content which can cause discomfort or illness that will cause further dehydration.

Water requirements are so critical to man's existence that Mountain Rescue volunteers always fill their canteens at home. They never rely upon nature to provide water, even from mountain streams. Water should be one item you always provide for in your pre-trip planning. And not only for your personal use — remember, automobiles also may require more water in hot environments. Digging for water is frustrating, exhausting and probably useless. Anyone going into obviously arid country must carry all the water he needs. That *extra five gallons of water may save your life.*

Helping Yourself to be Found in the Desert

Desert distances are deceiving, and one hill often looks just like another. That light you can see across the desert can be 20 or 30 miles away. Don't get itchy feet and try to walk out unless you know you are not going to be looked for by those back home. The surest way to be missed is: NEVER LEAVE CIVILIZATION WITHOUT TELLING SOMEONE WHERE YOU ARE GOING and approximately WHEN YOU PLAN TO RETURN.

If you do have a mechanical problem or become lost, you can let a lot of people know that you are in distress with signals. Signals, in effect, make you a distinctive speck on the desert rather than another clump of brush. Colorful clothing, tarps, or a bright colored vehicle can be seen for a long distance. Smoke by day and a bright fire by night are known distress signals.

Mirrors are very useful in signaling faroff vehicles and aircraft. Almost anything bright and shiny can be used as a mirror when used as shown in Figure 7. But practice aiming it before hand. Sweep the horizon periodically.

Mirror flashes can be seen long before you can see or hear the plane or vehicle. Aim flashes toward civilization. Check your map for direction.

Figure 7

To be found quickly, use every known method of making yourself effectively larger by signals.

Common Desert Problems

Too much heat in any form can cause humans a host of problems. Most outdoorsmen are aware that too much heat also affects the mechanical equipment they use for transportation, the majority of which are liquid cooled and may develop symptoms of overheating. Modern vehicles such as the Jeep, dune buggy, motorbike, snowmobile and automobile are all capable of getting up places they cannot get down, or down into places they cannot get out from. Getting stuck in the sand seems to be the most common desert problem, followed by overheated engines, flat tires, punctured gas tanks and oil pans. High-centering on rutted roads is common. Bent tie rods and many other mechanical problems can develop from travel on rough roads.

The vehicle is your best chance of getting back, so carry emergency repair tools (see Appendix for suggested list of tools and other items for automobile survival). It may save you having to wait several days for rescue.

It is not easy to sit and wait, when with a few tools you could improvise repairs to that vehicle and ride back home. You might have to go slowly, but it sure beats walking.

STAYING ALIVE IN AN EXTREME HEAT EMERGENCY

First Stage

Get out of direct sunlight into shade.

Analyze approximate length of emergency and chance of assistance.

Analyze immediate dangers:
Intensity of heat — time of day.
Environmental hazards.
Amount of water — amount of remaining energy.

Analyze resources:
Available water — food — clothing — shelter.
Emergency equipment — medicine — signals — transportation.

Stop or minimize all muscle action during intense heat period.

Cover the body with loose, lightweight cotton clothing, especially the neck and head.

Second Stage

Stay in shade, if possible. Get up off the hot ground.

Drink when thirsty. Stay salty. Don't eat — it causes more water loss.

Keep mouth shut — minimize talk — tongue may swell.

Analyze what the heat is doing to your body, then do everything possible to minimize its destructive force.

Improve your retention of body water.

Wear dark glasses. Do not remove clothing.

Don't travel cross country — unless absolutely necessary. You will get only 10 miles to the gallon of water.

Work or walk slowly — rest often.

Watch for symptoms of any of the heat problems — especially in older persons.

IMPROVISING

IMPROVISING LIFE SUPPORT ESSENTIALS

Whenever man leaves civilization (hiking) or civilization leaves man (disaster), man will be forced to live without the benefit of modern technology and governmental security. He will then be forced by circumstances to rely upon his own knowledge and decisions in protecting and providing for his wellbeing.

Man must understand that in any emergency he can and must improvise his basic needs from the materials available, both natural and man–made.

To survive in the wilderness, man may have to make tools like a cave man, dig into the earth and live like an animal and possibly forage like a scavenger for food and water.

The greatest problem in your survival will be keeping the body alive a little longer. Keeping the heart pumping, the brain thinking, the arms and legs capable of moving long enough to get out of your predicament. Money and equipment will be of little value if you cannot utilize it to help keep the body alive long enough to get out of your emergency situation.

Problem solving to improvise your necessities requires the mental capacity to reason, analyze and compare. Plus the determination to succeed.

While most emergencies are short-lived and require only temporary improvisations, all require adherence to the priorities of life and survival. Once you have determined a survival necessity, satisfy that need any way ethically possible.

This task may require a basic knowledge of physics, chemistry and psychology to bolster common sense practices. Sometimes this is known as ingenuity, or improvising. In reality, it is making something do something you need. It may not be perfect, but it may serve your purpose.

If you have ever participated in a brainstorming session, you are aware of the multitude of uses to which a particular item could be applied. They tell us that a small paper clip has over 100 potential uses besides holding papers together.

Improvising is the reverse of this type of brainstorming — to solve the problem or immediate need from all of the resources around you.

Improvising is making something serve a purpose to help you solve a problem. First, you have to recognize that you have a definite problem. Once you determine what you need, sit down and think. Think of all of the things that would satisfy that need. What does it really do that makes it different from other things? How does it accomplish this feat? What does it look like? What is it made of? What size should it be? Could it be made of other materials? How was it constructed? Have you ever seen it constructed differently? Could you use something different? Do you really need this, or could you manage to survive without it?

Once you decide you really need it, be positive! Now look around you, above, below you. Construct it from what materials are near you.

Classify your needs and give them priorities. Shelter, water, fire, clothing, food. Give them priorities so that you waste no time in false efforts. (Example: building a shelter too far from water or fire materials.)

The body's necessities and priorities are the same in the city or in the wilderness. Only the methods of how you acquire and prepare or construct them may differ. Air, shelter, water, warmth, and food — and the will to live — are the requirements. The will to live must be predominant in all situations for positive results in survival. Air and water may be polluted, creating a secondary problem of purifying or moving to another location free of contamination.

Since there will be so many variables that could affect your survival emergency this chapter will cover only the most important ones that might occur in wilderness areas.

Life is so dependent upon a constant internal temperature that body shelter must take top priority in storms or temperature extremes. A combination of wind with rain or cold can extract body heat faster than your body can produce it, on the other hand the sun and hot ground can cause heat gain faster than your body can dissipate it. In such cases, adequate protective shelter for the body is mandatory for survival.

Shelter in the city comes in thousands of varieties. Some good, some not so good. Some are portable, such as cars, campers, trucks, etc. Homes vary in size from cardboard shacks to mansions — basements to penthouses. Each uses different methods and materials to provide a floor, walls, and roof over your head. But basically, they shelter your body from the hostile elements.

Natural environments may contain the same materials — only in a different shape or form. Trees furnish lumber for the city builder, who has the tools to reshape it. You may not have tools, so you must use the trees' debris, duff, limbs, bark, or fallen trees for construction materials. The shape of material is incidental as long as it performs the task you desire. Natural masonry materials are everywhere — rocks, sand, mud, dirt, snow, ice may be used, the same way a city mason would build something.

There are hundreds of ways to build a shelter for your body. What works for wind may not be adequate for rain. What shelters the body from the sun may not be of much help in the cold. But if you know the principles of house building, insulation, radiation, conduction, convection, you may be able to find suitable natural building materials to improvise adequate body shelter.

Basic natural and man-made materials may include anything movable or attainable that you can stack, tie, nail, break, fashion or utilize to serve your need. Paper or cardboard, cartons, maps; wood, lumber — even the doghouse offers protection; metal, plastic, rugs, mats; rocks, bricks, ice, snow; trees, logs, caves, dens.

Some survival trainees have used rotten log chunks as building blocks. Others used slabs of bark off the large downed logs to make excellent non-conductive floors, walls, and roofs. History tells of storm-bound pioneers wearing slab bark clothing. There is no end to what you can make out of natural materials if you look about you.

Forest Shelter:

"What do you look for in the forest?" is the question most often asked of survival instructors. Their advice is to look for anything that is already half built. Such as a fallen tree that has a crawl space with good drainage — one you can make larger easily, to save energy. Look around for bark, trees, green boughs, limbs, or an old, dry, rotten log for building blocks; flat, stackable rocks; or loose dirt.

Once you have found a possible site for your shelter, look up, down, and around the site. Any potential dangers — dead trees that may fall down in the wind? Avalanche chute, rockfall, dry wash? How about the wind direction and exposure? Could you have a safe, small fire inside or outside your shelter?

How about construction tools? What can you see? The answer to that is, use anything you have. Saw, axe, hard hat, mess kit, spoon, green limb, flat wood, stones — or if you have to, use your fingers as claws. Be careful, now. Avoid any injury. Even a scratch may compound your problem tomorrow.

The first stage of construction is to enlarge the crawl space however you can. Work slowly to avoid perspiring; it costs body water and energy. Make the space big enough to stretch out your legs, if possible. You will have to exercise leg and arm muscles to produce body heat. Push the dirt out to form the wall bases. Keep the space as small as possible to make less air space to heat with your body heat. When you look at your shelter now, you have a roof, a floor, and possibly two or more walls.

The second stage is to gather thick bark for a sub-floor and for the outer walls. If it is raining, use the tile roof method to channel the water down the side. If not, use the shingling method, by starting at the bottom and overlapping each layer of bark. Save one large chunk of bark for a door-way. If no bark is handy, use sticks or dead wood and cover with a thick layer of duff or dirt. Use small brush limbs to bind and hold the dirt on the wall. The door helps the mind ward off real or imaginary furious animals during the night.

The third stage is insulating the floor from conduction heat loss. This is a must. Try to find the driest bark, dead wood, or thickest boughs to sit or lie on. Try to find material that has a low heat conduction factor.

Fourth stage — Crawl in and try it out. It should be slightly cramped and uncomfortable. That's all right. It isn't quite as good as home, but temporary shelters rarely are. Rest a moment and think about how you can improve it. Plan to chink the holes before dark. If your bed is damp, find drier insulation. You must do everything possible to stay dry. Think about warmth, fire, and fire fuel. Do you really need fire? Your body is a fantastic furnace and will heat a good, closed shelter quite adequately.

Clothing:

Clothing is a shelter you wear close to your body to control the body's internal and radiated environment from the natural environment. There are few places on earth that the human body does not need some extra pro-tection from the sun, heat, wind, cold, or rain. The prime purpose of this protection is to help maintain a near constant internal body temperature. If you do not have clothing sufficient to protect the inner body temperature, you must improvise some other type of temporary body shelter that supports what you already have. There is a multitude of materials that may be used as substitute clothing.

In emergency situations, improvising must be accomplished from existing fabrics and materials you happen to have near you. When your pants are falling down for lack of a belt, your choice of something to hold them up may run from sacrificed equipment like shoelaces, yarn, or pack materials to natural material (like vines, green limbs) to man-made articles from cars and aircraft (such as wire, plastic, or rubber). If you need clothing to supplement what you already have, consider anything that is cuttable, bendable, pliable, and fastenable. Material should be large enough to minimize fastening pieces together.

Consider why you need it — what's the problem?

Wetness —   Consider water-proof materials.

Cold —   Consider conductivity of the material.

Heat —   Consider conductivity of the material.

Wind —   Consider porosity and conductivity.

A few of the possible materials are: fabric, paper, cardboard, plastic, rugs, rubber, skins, insulation, bark, wood. Think. Any of these could be improvised into body shelter.

Sewing your improvised clothing: Look about you. If you need a button, try a sharp bone or stick. The problem is some way to hold two pieces of material together. For the needle to sew with, use anything that will put a small hole through the material. Sure, it will take some time to sew yourself a pair of overboots and mittens. But you have time, or should take time if this vital to your survival.

Anything bendable and cuttable, that is small in diameter, will suffice for sewing improvised clothing. Vehicles use lots of wire, which works fine for sewing the heavy materials such as seat covers, floor mats, maps, rubber, etc. Green vines, roots or the inner bark layers of trees are strong and can be found, cut, and shaped to serve as twine.

Be practical. Look for substitute improvising supplies from man-made items you carry or have near you first. It is surprising how many outdoorsmen never utilize everything they have with them. Look, think, then look again. In survival situations, everything is expendable to save your life.

Water Procurement:

Your body cannot tolerate a water deficiency for very long. Water needs are determined by the muscle work load, ambient temperature, humidity, amount of solar heat, and your clothing and shelter. If all of the preceding are near the normal levels, your body should be able to last from three to four days without water.

This means that you should search for water to build your shelter near. If none is near, improvise water catch basins in the dirt for rain and dew. Search for green vegetation, or moss, or water-holding plants, such as barrel cactus. Water procurement may not be easy, even after finding wet ground. You may have to wring the water out the moss, or dig several catch basins for the seepage water.

You may find water by digging in likely areas, but it depends upon such a host of variables that it often is not worth the water loss, energy loss to gain it. Conserving what water you have inside the body and protecting that extra supply are far more practical.

Keep water covered to prevent evaporation. Never leave water bottles uncapped or emergency containers unclosed. There is too great a chance the precious water may spill.

Carrying your water when you travel is a problem. When using plastic, rubber, or glass, try to protect it from punctures or breakage with extra clothes. Try to improvise lids for any metal containers used to carry water.

Purifying water is advisable whenever there is doubt of its purity. Boiling for 3 to 4 minutes, drops of iodine, special water purification tablets, or certain household chlorine preparations may be used. Most water-borne diseases are curable with medication, so it is advisable to drink any water rather than go without if the need is critical. You should seek medical aid and advice of a doctor as soon as you return to civilization.

Watch the birds and animals around water holes. If they do not drink water, it should be assumed to be contaminated or poisonous. Animals leave trails in their daily search for water. Birds fly to water in the evening and morning. Follow them if water procurement is a problem.

If you are fortunate and find a source of water, stay near it. Carry as much as you can if you must travel. In arid areas, water procurement takes time.

SIMPLE VEGETATION WATER STILL

This is a quick and easy way to get water if you have a large, clear plastic bag and available desert vegetation, such as cactus, brush, grass, etc.

Scoop out a crater-like hole (size determined by bag size) on a sloping dune or built-up mound. Place the plastic bag over the crater, bag opening on the down-slope side. Use a stick or something to make a tent over the crater. Place clean rocks or weights around the outer crater rim to hold the plastic tent taut. Fill the crater hole with vegetation. Use care not to have any vegetation outside the hole or touching the plastic. As soon as the vegetation warms up, water will condense on the inside of the plastic, and droplets will run down the tent to the outside of the crater.

Form a sand trough down-slope from the crater to a catch hole or pool for the condensed water. Close the plastic bag tight and wait in the shade. To get water out of the bag, scoop a deeper hole just below your catch pool. Open the plastic bag just a little bit and pour out the condensed water. Do not drink the water the vegetation sat in in the crater.

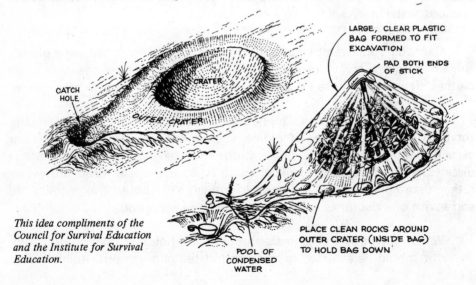

CATCH HOLE

CRATER

OUTER CRATER

LARGE, CLEAR PLASTIC BAG FORMED TO FIT EXCAVATION

PAD BOTH ENDS OF STICK

PLACE CLEAN ROCKS AROUND OUTER CRATER (INSIDE BAG) TO HOLD BAG DOWN

POOL OF CONDENSED WATER

This idea compliments of the Council for Survival Education and the Institute for Survival Education.

Clear plastic is best, yellow or a semi-transparent color next best. Dark colored plastic blocks out the sun's rays, and slows condensation.

Do not open the still unless necessary, because it takes a long time for it to regain its operating atmosphere. Since the solar still takes time, it is advisable to set it up to work while you are resting in the shade. If you have the materials make several stills.

Food Procurement:

Finding edible foods in the wilderness is relatively easy. Cooking and preparing them may pose a problem to someone without fire for heat or a pot to cook his edible plants. Learning what plants to eat and which to avoid is a separate subject that is too complex to be included in this book. Food is far down on the list of body priorities during short-term emergencies. Conservation of what energy you have with you at the time is far more important.

Unfamiliar foods may cause stomach problems worse than doing without. Some natural foods must be boiled and reboiled several times for safety. Each different area requires different identification handbooks.

There are many variables in selecting natural foods, but the following are a few rules that may be useful.

Most seeds are edible, if cooked.

Most roots are edible, if cooked.

Most blue colored berries are edible.

Anything that swims, crawls, flies, or walks has edible muscle portions.

Beware of plants with milky sap.

Beware of any plants or mushrooms you cannot positively identify.

At least 75% of the inexperienced students taking survival courses desire knowledge of edible plants. After completing the course most of these students recognize the fact the food procurement costs energy, time, and equipment. It may cost more energy than you can replace from the edible material you find. Abundant natural food is a seasonal commodity. Wariness of poisonous plants may cause unknown food to bring more concern than comfort. What grows at one place may not grow in another. Each temperature zone has different plant and animal life. Each elevation has different plant life.

IS IT SAFE TO EAT   ???   It is --- It isn't   It is -- It isn't   It is -- Well maybe.

Warmth:

In some cold areas you must have artificial heat to gain any measure of comfort. The type and size of the shelter, quality of materials used, and workmanship will determine the true need of fire for warmth. The better the shelter, the less need for fire.

Think of the animals. They don't have fire and they live in this same environment. Remember the sleeping bag principle. It is two layers of fabric separated by a layer of fluffy fibers. Your body produces the heat within the insulated sleeping area. The same principle should be applied to improvised shelters. The smaller, drier, and better insulated it is, the less heat loss and the less need for fire.

Should you determine you definitely need fire for warmth or for psychological comfort, keep it small in size. The Indians' axiom was, "White man builds big fire, keeps warm gathering wood." Fire will consume fuel in proportion to its size. Also, the danger increases with size.

Think about all of the ways you might be able to gain warmth: bundling, cuddling people, live animals — dogs, horses, or cattle. A lighted candle or lantern might raise the temperature of a good shelter a few degrees. Warm sand, heated rocks, will hold the heat for several hours of comfortable rest.

FAMOUS LAST WORDS

"I wish I had brought
a coat and some
long pants."

Improvising fire for warmth and cooking:

Modern technology has relieved most of you from the chore of starting. stoking and banking the home's heating and cooking fires. It also has done away with the necessity of personal involvement in fuel procurement. This cutting, splitting, storage of adequate fuel was a never-ending chore for the pioneers. They knew what fuel to use to start the fire; which fuels burned slowly and hot; which produce smoke and which burned fast, plus a host of other facts about when to cut and how to store their fuel. They had to — their lives depended upon this knowledge.

Most people today can start a fire if they have enough chemical fire starters or the Sunday newspaper to support their effort. But in an emergency, the chances are you may not even have a match. Even if you have a match, tests show that 5 out of 20 persons cannot get a small fire started in dry conditions. Most often the reason for failure is *impatience, inexperience,* and *poor selection* of the starter fuels. Fire building is an art that requires some basic knowledge of why a fire burns and which fuels have a low incendiary coefficient.

Fire building can be important to your survival. It provides warmth, dries clothing, gives light, lifts the morale, is required for cooking, and it makes an excellent signalling device. Despite all of the above good points, fire can kill and destroy if it becomes uncontrolled. There are times, because of this danger, that a fire should not be started, i.e., on close to dry, flammable materials, explosive substances, in a very dry grassland, or in a forest that smells resinous. Sometimes the forests become so dry and the air so full of resin fumes that it seems like a turpentine factory, where one match might cause total conflagration.

You cannot outrun a forest fire or a grass fire. So use caution in selection of the site to start your fire.

What is a safe fire area? A place away from flammable materials. Away from overhanging burnable materials. Where the mineral soil is free of grass, duff and roots. Free from wind gusts.

Once you decide you want a fire, determine if it is safe to start a fire. Select a safe place — near water, if possible. Look around your site. Do you have fuel nearby?

Fire pit construction:

Scratch down to mineral earth that is free of forest duff, grass and roots, an area approximately five to six feet in diameter. In the center of this circle construct a fire retainer of rocks. (Bear in mind that river stones often contain moisture and may explode when heated.) If no rocks are available, consider a pit fire or trench fire. A trench fire is almost a must in windy areas.

FACE
OPENINGS
CROSS WIND

10 to 12"

Finding fuel for the fire:

Gather all necessary dry burnable materials before hand. It pays to select the driest tinder, kindling and fuel possible. Look in old hollow logs, dead stumps and dead limbs on living trees. Look for twigs and limbs up off the damp ground. Sometimes the only dry wood will be in the heart of old stumps and downed logs. Nearly always you can find small dry twigs next to the trunks of larger trees. Old stumps that have a single spire protruding from the middle core usually contain pitch wood. The reason the spire did not rot away like the rest of the stump is because that small section is full of pitch and does not deteriorate as fast as the soft wood part of the stump. Pitch wood is so full of resin that it makes excellent fire starting material.

For your fire to burn it must have three ingredients: oxygen, heat and fuel. A shortage of any one and the fire will not burn properly.

OXYGEN

FUEL

HEAT

Initial Heat Source: Even the driest tinder needs heat or flame for ignition. Wood matches, petroleum lighters, paper matches, are the best. Since a match flame is short-lived, the match should be used to light a candle or shave stick to prolong the life span of the initial flame to be applied to the tinder and kindling. There are many substitutes for matches in fire starting: friction, magnifying lens, battery sparks. Flint and steel are still used to start fine, fuzzy tinder. The secret of using them is in your ability to toss the spark into the tinder. Scraping a knife blade across a hard rock also may make sparks. Any convex lens from a camera or binoculars can be used in bright sunlight to focus the sun's rays on the tinder. High voltage batteries can produce a spark arc that may be used to light fire tinder or a fuel dampened rag. As a last resort, try rubbing two sticks together. It can be done, using the right type of wood, spindle, bowstring, and lot of persistence.

After gathering fire fuel

Make three piles	Tinder	All fuel must be gathered before
	Kindling	attempting to start the fire.
	Fuel	Keep all dry in wet weather.

Tinder should be a handful of extremely flammable material to receive the initial flame or heat source. Pitch, dry grass, lint, cotton fuzz, wood shavings, hair, paper, inner bark of birch, cedar, steel wool, petroleum products, shaved sticks, candle, oil wick.

Kindling is something that will ignite easily from the tinder or base flame. This fuel should be broken, split, or shaved to increase flammability. Pitch wood (undecayed spires on old stumps) Squaw wood (small dead twigs on trees) or any dry wood of pencil size.

Fuel may be anything that will not burn readily from the initial flame. Such as: Dead wood (finger size to leg size) Dried dung, dry peat, coal, plastic, fabric, rubber, oil, and green wood.

Arrange the tinder in such a manner that your heat source (tinder or flame) rises through the maximum amount of kindling. A teepee shape is best. When the kindling begins to burn and generate its own heat add the next larger sized pieces of fuel. When this fuel begins to catch on fire add the larger, longer lasting wood or fuel.

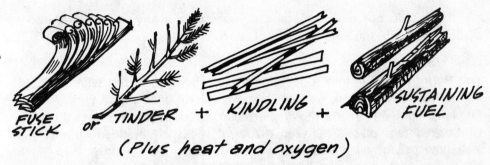

FUSE STICK or TINDER + KINDLING + SUSTAINING FUEL

(Plus heat and oxygen)

The greatest error novice firestarters make is smothering the tiny kindling flame with too much fuel too soon. This loss of draft with its vital oxygen quickly snuffs the flame. Impatience is another common error. Speedy fuel selection, fire setting and match striking can be foolhardy. One match fire building is an art, that should be practiced often. History tells of men using lots of paper money trying to start wet fuel. Others have searched in vain for dry kindling and ended up using a piece of dry shirt tail as fire starter for the little dry wood they had.

Fire without wood fuel

A gasoline stove for heat, signaling, or cooking may be improvised from a metal can. Make draft and smoke holes on the sides then fill the can 1/3 full of dry dirt or sand. Saturate the sand with a little gasoline. Wait a few moments for the excess fuel vapors to escape. Then light the fuel with a tossed match. After the initial puff the sand will settle down to an even flame. Stir the sand occasionally to bring fresh fuel/sand to the surface.

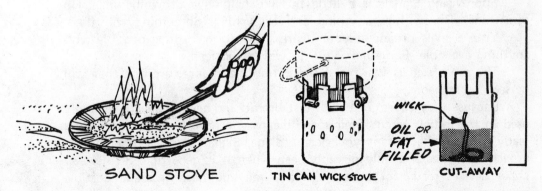

SAND STOVE   TIN CAN WICK STOVE   WICK — OIL OR FAT FILLED — CUT-AWAY

If you do not have a metal can you can pour any volatile fuel into a shallow hole in the dirt or sand. Use rocks to support your cook pot.

Wick stoves

Pour heavy oil into a metal can. Improvise a cotton wick about 4 inches long and support part of it above the oil with a bent wire. Animal fat, lard, light oil or any heavy petroleum product may be used this way. Oil soaked rags placed between a row of rocks or shredded upholstry in a shallow pan of oil will burn.

Fire building problems:

Keeping a fire from sinking into deep snow will require a platform of some material to insulate the fire from melting the snow. Metal on green logs or green logs criss-crossed. See Illustration

Signals

Improvising Signals is a little bit like helping a drowning man. Do something! Throw him anything and everything. Something will float.

Your signals broadcast your distress. So do everything possible with anything available. Something you do will be noticed.

The more signals you make the better the chances are that they will be seen by someone.

Because they cover great areas fast, aircraft and helicopters are generally used in the initial search. Their speed means you have to have your signals ready for use the instant you hear a plane. Signals are best seen by approaching planes and only possibly seen when it is departing. So have *all signal* devices ready for instant use anytime you hear or see a possible searcher. Stay near set signals that need lighting or manipulating.

Standard Signals:

The international distress signals are 3 loud sounds of any kind repeated at intervals or 3 fires set in a large equilateral triangle. Voice distress is Mayday, Mayday, Mayday or S.O.S.

Signal devices:

Flares, radios, dye, panels, flags, lights, rockets, horns, mirrors and emergency radio beepers are a few of the commercially available signal devices. But in the field smoke, light flashes, fires, sounds, color or shadows will attract attention.

If you are certain searchers are looking for you, do anything possible to change the surrounding landscape. In brush, cut conspicous patterns in the vegetation, on the snow; tramp large side trenches or pile brush or rocks to spell out your message — S.O.S. — H.E.L.P.

Try to place these trenches or piles so the sun will create shadows for emphasis. The key is to do something to make an obvious contrast to the normal scene.

Signal Fires and other signals:

Smoke by day and fire by night are always good signals because of the great distance they can be seen and the fact that Smokey the Bear is looking for these all the time.

Trees tend to disperse smoke so try to place signal fires in the open. On a clear day or over light colored terrain such as sand or snow, try to use black smoke by adding rubber, coated fabric, plastic or oil to your signal fire. On a dark cloudy day or over dark colored brush or vegetation use white smoke. Add green boughs, grass, leaves, duff or wet cloth to a hot signal fire.

Mirror flashes or reflections have saved many lives. You can reflect sunlight from mirrors, shiny metal or unpolished metal coated with grease. You can hand rub polish soft metals. See illustration on page 74 on the simplified method of using a mirror. Use is limited by the weather but will work without full sunlight. Sweep the horizon constantly.

Color is vital to attract attention. White airplanes down on the snow or green airplanes in the forest are nearly impossible to see. Search observers remind us that they can only see the bright colors like yellow, orange, light red, and white down among green vegetation. So if you are wearing green, brown, blue or any dark color, maybe you should change. Use your white underclothes as flags or change the showing color with dye or paint. Small signal panels or flags are more easily seen if they move slowly or wave. Animals and birds sit still to hide. If they move you notice them. Moving provides the needed contrast from the normal.

If you have flares, two way radios, or other signal devices, use them only during that time of the day when they will be most noticable. Small radios and emergency beepers have range limitations that require high ground for maximum effectiveness. Use them at the time most listeners might be listening such as 4 to 9 P.M.

Ground to air signals tell the story of your distress. The following are a few of those most useful and easily remembered.

| Require doctor — serious injury | Require medical supplies | Require food and water | Am proceeding in this direction | No — negative | Yes — affirmative | All well | Unable to proceed |

Repeated sounds coming from unusual places or at odd times always attract attention. Whistles, drums, gunshots. Anything audible such as a big stick on the side of a metal plane or a hollow log can carry a vital message in an emergency. If you don't have a whistle make one out of a sapling. Yelling or shouting should be used only when you hear the ground party close to you.

Signal Tips

If you are traveling try to stay in or near the open areas with bright colored signals handy. Also leave a note, or signal of your direction of travel, in case your original signals are found.

Stay near man-made equipment whenever possible because of the enormous supply of usable materials for signals, shelters, fire and insulation.

If in the water, enlarge your silhouette any way possible. Use a flotsom stick with a colored flag on it. In deep vegetation it might be wise to extend a flag above the tops to increase your chances of being noticed.

Signalling, like anything else in survival, must be accomplished without further danger to yourself. It must contribute to bettering your chances of being found alive or it will have been a waste of energy.

Analyze every action for effectiveness and danger of injury. *Caution as well as Contrast* is the watch word in improvising signalling needs.

RULES FOR IMPROVISING

If you know the problem and evaluate it, the solution is usually easy to attain. In improvising a need — THINK! "Your brain is your best survival tool." A need is usually something you are used to having and using.

What was it?
How did it work?
What was it made of?
What was its basic function?
What were its basic movements?
How was it constructed?

Now think like a caveman or pioneer — What did they use to fulfill this basic need? What is your basic need? What is in your immediate vicinity that may be used to fulfill this need?

Will it work?
Could you modify it?
What will make it work?

If that doesn't work, what will?
Think about it
Touch it
Move it
Imagine it
Experiment
Change it
Fix it
Work it
— It's done! It serves your need.

If it still doesn't work — TRY AGAIN. Your life may need it.

A MAN WHO THINKS HE CAN SURVIVE WILL SURVIVE

For example, you need a knife to cut with. A knife is a sharp piece of metal — or a sharp object. What do you have that is metal (coin, belt buckle, key, button, can, ring, pen, pack, compass, hair clip, etc.)? What does Nature provide (sharp edged rocks, splintered hardwood, thorns, ice)?

How can you sharpen these? By flattening with a rock, grinding on a flat rock, chipping, rubbing together, heating and pounding, breaking, etc.

By thinking basic, caveman style, you have improvised a tool that will cut.

INTERESTING CLOTHING EXPERIMENTS

Most experienced outdoorsmen advise tenderfeet to wear loose fitting wool clothing. If you doubt their advice, try this experiment:

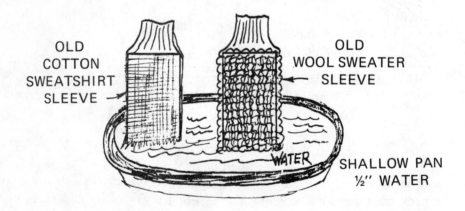

OLD COTTON SWEATSHIRT SLEEVE →

← OLD WOOL SWEATER SLEEVE

WATER

SHALLOW PAN ½″ WATER

The water will wick up the cotton very quickly and remain wet. The wool gets wet where it is in the water. Wool has the unique property of retaining body warmth even when wet — dries quickly, and sheds water. The same wicking happens when you walk across a wet meadow and get your knees wet.

Hypothermia (killer of the unprepared) is caused by accidental lowering of the body temperature during wet, windy or cold conditions. Lack of proper clothing, inadequate shelter and energy depletion are the most common contributors to serious problems during stormy weather.

Try this simple demonstration:

Get four 2-gallon metal cans. Dress three of them: one in wool, one in cotton, and one in cotton and wool with plastic shelter; leave one bare. Fill all four with 110° hot water. Place all cans in a shaded, windy spot outdoors. Record their temperatures each hour. Radiation, convection and conduction will remove the heat very rapidly and simulate their effect on the human body under similar conditions. This experiment has startled many persons because of the speed that one can lose its heat.

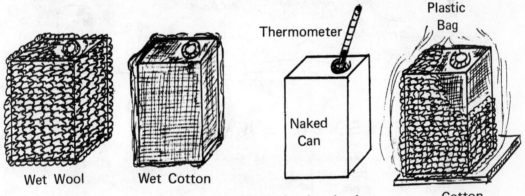

Wet Wool　　　　Wet Cotton

Thermometer

Naked Can

Plastic Bag

Cotton & Wool

Put all 4 cans through a sprinkler-simulated rainstorm

SURVIVAL EXPERIMENTS

The ideal way to practice survival is to get in your car and travel into the back country. Find a wooded area along some lonely backroad, away from houses and civilization. Take along only matches, a knife and the clothing that you are wearing. Travel 100 to 200 feet into the woods and set up your survival camp. If you cannot adapt to the situation and improvise your needs, you can walk back to your car and go home. This is one way you can experience the psychological and physiological problems that accompany a survival situation.

Overnight emergency provisions you can fabricate in a few minutes at home from kitchen and garage supplies.

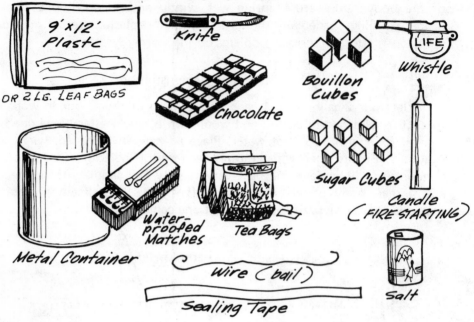

PERSONAL SURVIVAL KIT

A suitable container may be found in a pint turpentine or thinner can which has been thoroughly cleaned and dried. Cut the top off and remove sharp burrs.

Put all small items in plastic sandwich bags to keep them dry. Add bandaids, medication, spare prescription lens, needle and thread, safety pins, and other small vital necessities.

In just a few minutes you can assemble and package the components of this kit so that you may be prepared for a short-term emergency situation. To reseal the can, fashion a lid from plastic and tape securely in place.

Such a kit, homemade or purchased, cannot help you survive a storm unless it is available when needed. Always carry it whenever you travel away from civilization.

AUTOMOBILE SURVIVAL KIT

(Components of this vital kit may be found in most homes and garages.)

Your vehicle is your movable , second home.

Always carry a few items for use during delays, emergencies or mechanical failures.

EMERGENCY EQUIPMENT for COMFORT, SAFETY,and LIFE SUPPORT.

Carry these in your trunk or glove compartment the year around:

Sun glasses	Colored plastic tarp (9 x 12)
Spare tire, jack, tire change tools	Water bucket
Tire chains that fit	Multiple screwdriver set
Heavy rope or tow cable	Crescent wrench
Signal aids — flashlight, flares	Pliers, slip joint
Shovel (short garden spade)	Pliers, vise grip
Pruning saw or axe	Roll of electrical tape
Small file	6' of soft steel wire

Small kit of assorted nuts, bolts, small springs, nails, etc.

Old pair of individual's prescription glasses.

PERSONAL COMFORT and SAFETY, or LIFE SUPPORT:

Woolen blanket or sleeping bag	Chocolate bars (4 or 5)
Freezable liquids (diet food drinks)	Small cans of fruit (303 size)
Dry foods (crackers, ryecrisp, etc.)	Matches (for fire)

Put all dry foods in a 3-lb. coffee can, which can also serve as an emergency stove or water container

In vehicles being used for outdoor activities, walking shoes and a complete change of old, usable clothing is advised, as well as a rain coat.

AUTOMOBILE FIRST AID KIT

Sealable plastic container,	Scissors
2 Compress bandages	Bar Soap
1 Triangle bandage	Tube of Foile (for burns)
Small roll of 2" tape	Ampoule of ammonia inhalants
6 — 3 x 3 gauze pads	Green soap disinfectant
25 Aspirins	Needle
10 Bandaids	Safety pins
Knife.	Matches

In vehicle survival---- Always drive defensively-- Think ahead, use self talk and psycho-pictography to visualize potential dangers to self and vehicle.

STALLED VEHICLE and EMERGENCY PROCEDURES
If Away From Civilization

Your vehicle is a moving shelter, designed to move you and yours from one place to another. In an emergency, knowledge and improvisation can keep you moving closer to home or help. 5 MPH is not very fast, but it is better than walking during a storm.

Damaged and leaky radiator (emergency only): Plug hole with rags, wood, material. Using cream of wheat, Wheateena or other expanding wheat cereals mixed into radiator water can plug hole from the inside.

Leak in water hoses to heater. Disconnect both ends and plug with limb or wood. Retighten clamps

Leak in a water hose on engine. Plug hole; wrap with cloth, then electrical tape. Remove radiator cap to relieve water pressure. Keep engine rpm low.

Punctured hole in gas tank can be sealed with bar soap carved to fit hole.

Broken hydraulic brake lines can be crimped between the leak and the hydraulic pump. Use low gear to help stop.

Vapor lock can happen to overheated engines in vehicles which are traveling slowly or pulling up steep hills in high altitudes. This is usually caused by overheated fuel lines near the engine. The gasoline liquid turns to a vapor, causing a bubble that stops the flow of liquid. The symptoms of vapor lock are the same as out of fuel. Cool all fuel lines, carburetor, fuel pump with wet rags and ventilation. If you suspect a flooded carburetor (engine compartment smells of gasoline) during starting, push the accelerator to the floor and hold. Do not pump the accelerator.

To extend the miles you can travel when low on fuel, slow down to 25 or 35 MPH. Coast downhill when possible. Shift down a gear when it is necessary to use full throttle. Keep RPM steady; 1500 to 2000 is best.

It is better to creep along in a limping auto at 5 MPH than to walk home in a storm of wind, rain, or heat.

Loss of traction in sand, mud, snow: Weight distribution is often the major problem. Transfer of weight to drive wheels (adding weight — rocks, snow, wood, sand, people) will give traction enough to get over a hill. Too much weight in one spot can alter vehicle's steering characteristics. Floor mats can be used to give short distance traction.

If car is snowbound during a storm and you cannot see a house or light nearby, prepare to stay in the car. A window must be opened enough to allow oxygen to enter. In extreme emergencies (when you are in danger of freezing) consider the door and ceiling insulation, maps, etc., as material to help keep you warm. The smaller the nest, the easier it will be to keep warm. As a last resort, use seats to make sleeping bag, using electrical wire for sewing upholstery.

CAUTION: Cars can be airtight, so allow ventilation for carbon dioxide and possible carbon monoxide. If you leave a snowbound vehicle, leave a note as to your destination and condition.

DESERT TRAVEL

Extra water is advised. Cleaned bleach jugs can serve as emergency water canteens.

Getting stuck in the sand seems to be the greatest desert driving problem; it is advised you carry 6' of mesh fencing and a few short 2 x 12 planks to support the car jack for lifting. In emergency, use floor mats to give support and traction, or hub caps for jack support.

PRIVATE AIRCRAFT — DOWNED AIRCRAFT — LIFE SUPPORT KIT
(Components of this vital kit may be found in most homes and garages.)

Container — Any lightweight metal container with lid, suitable to heat and store water.

Life Support Tools:
- Hack saw — Single handle with wood blade and metal blade
- Plier — vise grip
- Plier — slip joint
- Screwdriver set (multiple)

First Aid Kit — Personal:
- Sealable Plastic Container
- 2 — Compress bandages
- 1 — Triangle bandage
- Small roll 2" tape
- 6 — 3 x 3 gauze pads
- 25 — Aspirin
- 10 — Bandaids
- Razor blade or scissors
- Hotel size soap
- L — purse size
- Kleenex — purse size, or toilet paper
- 6 — Safety pins
- 1 — Small tube of Unguentine or Foile

Food and Energy Package — 1 man 5-day rations
- 2 or 3 cans of Sego, Nutriment or Metrecal for liquid and energy.
- 30 — sugar cubes — wrapped
- 10 — pilot bread or 25 crackers
- 10 — packets of salt
- 3 — tea bags
- 12 rock candy
- 5 — gum
- 10 — bouillon cubes
- 20 — protein wafers (if available)

Shelters (minimum of 2):
- Large plastic sheets — 9' x 12' — Heavy gauge (one for each person) colored red or yellow preferred for signal panels

Life Support Kit:
- Waterproofed matches
- Candle or fire starter
- Signal mirror
- Compass — small
- Knife — Boy Scout style
- Insect repellent
- Mosquito net
- 50'-1/8" nylon rope or shroud line
- Whistle
- Smoke flares or red day-nite flares
- Radio Emergency Locator Beacon
- Radio -- Transceiver, 2 way

Use poly bags for water storage. Put each item in small plastic bag and seal. Put everything in small metal can (cook pot), seal with poly bag and tape.

DOWNED AIRCRAFT EMERGENCY PROCEDURES

A search normally starts after you are reported missing and your fuel is exhausted.

Stay away from the aircraft, if possible, until engines have cooled and spilled gasoline has evaporated.

Check for injuries, give first aid when necessary. Be careful in removing casualties from aircraft, particularly people with serious injuries.

Get out of wind and rain. Make or find temporary shelter.

Get your emergency signaling devices ready and have signal equipment handy. Every possible effort must be made to attract searchers to your location by signals — mirror, smoke, flares, color panels — and to sustain life and energy until assistance arrives.

Evaluate your location dangers: fire, sliding, rockfall, avalanche, terrain, weather.

Turn on or make sure your EMERGENCY LOCATOR BEACON is on

Search the aircraft for small personal items, tools, maps, etc.; evaluate and store for later use. Save everything. Keep dry.

> *Your prime effort must be directed toward conserving the energy you have.*

Stay with the aircraft if at all possible. It contains the basic ingredients for warmth, shelter and signaling materials.

Aircraft should be made VISIBLE FROM THE AIR if possible. Clear brush, cut trees, etc. Be prepared to make signals as aircraft approaches your area. Keep the mirror handy if the sun is shining. Practice its use.

Colored panels can tell a message. Pile brush is SOS. Stamp large, two-feet-wide letters SOS in the snow. Fill stamped marks with boughs or small brush.

Keep your signal fire burning all the time. Smoke and firelight can be seen from great distances. Both air and ground searchers will be looking for them.

Do not neglect your aircraft radio. It is possible it may still be operational. Turn squelch and volume; if you get any sound when mike button is pushed on and off it is possible that your radio is operational. Voice broadcast on a local frequency (in pilot's book) every 15 minutes during good weather — or if battery is weak, Morse Code SOS. Repeat often.

In cold weather, insulation and upholstery from the craft make excellent material for over-boots, sleeping bags, mittens, hats, and ground insulation. Sew them together with salvaged aircraft wire. Put plastic side out for better wetness protection.

Clear window makes fair emergency mirror. *Signals make you effectively bigger.*

Wings, rudder, etc., all may be used to make a shelter. Keep this shelter as small as possible, to lessen the area your body must heat. Insulate shelters with boughs, bark, tarps, maps, etc. Use *anything* to keep the wind and rain from getting inside your shelter. Body heat loss is energy lost.

Gasoline and engine oil are fuels for emergency heaters and stoves.

Your aircraft can fulfill most of your basic needs if you improvise. Think basic needs: Shelter (cover), warmth (fabric), tools (metal). Maps, newspaper, engine cover, plastic tarps all make excellent emergency bedding.

If running water is not readily available melt snow or ice in improvised pot, or squeegie (with windshield wiper, etc.) dew drops from aircraft surfaces. In an emergency, toss a sheet of flat plastic out the window so that it may collect dew or condensation. If it is raining, place plastic sheet in ground depression to collect water.

NAVIGATION

Walking or riding away from civilization means leaving street signs, roads, and familiar landmarks.

It is easy to walk away from a vehicle parked on a logging road in the back country. The real challenge is to walk back to that particular vehicle in fog, stormy weather, or dense timber. To do this requires a lot of luck or the use of navigation knowledge.

Trail hikers have less of a problem getting back than do wild game hunters, traveling cross country. At least the trail they hike may lead to some place, if only to the end of it — and back. Hunters follow a "hunch" across country in search of elusive animals. Cross country travel can end anywhere including unexpected and unfamiliar territory.

Experienced outdoorsmen who have learned the hard way will advise you to carry and learn to use map and compass. Land management agencies believe maps may aid travelers and they distribute millions of free maps to help visitors plan and travel across their land. Millions of free maps — yet most lost persons did not bother to pick up one or learn how to use it properly.

People who accidentally become lost, confused, or disoriented impose a costly burden on the agencies. Lost person searches take time, manpower, and money. The money is of minor significance when compared to the anxiety, worry and frustration for loved ones and family.

Being lost is not dangerous, in itself. In fact, it is quite a stimulating experience. As long as no emergency exists where time is critical, being lost is only a delaying side trip into strange places you might never see or visit.

No need to take notes while lost — you'll never forget the time or the place. Some old-timers would like to get lost, but they can't break the habit of knowing where they are all the time.

Every weekend thousands of novices and experienced outdoorsmen are in the back country, hoping one of their companions can navigate the way to the destination and back. They just follow. By always following, they save themselves the trouble of learning the art of navigation.

If the moral of that escapes you, consider yourself in a time-injury situation. All alone. Lost!! Now you are dependent upon your own brand of navigation and will live or perish by it. The real problem facing you is to stay alive long enough to trial and error your way back to camp.

The navigation necessary to travel in the wilderness is easy to learn and does not need to be exacting. You are not a surveyor, interested in exact land measurements. You are interested in finding the right canyon, road, trail, or river that is near your camp or vehicle. However, it does become an exacting challenge when you have a serious injury in your party. Now, time is of the utmost importance, and so is the exact location for rescue by land or air.

You must be able to

1. Travel out of the wilderness by the fastest route.
2. Report the problem to the sheriff or ranger.
3. Give a detailed report of the victim's condition.
4. Pinpoint the victim's exact location.
5. Report details necessary for land or air rescue.
6. If you cannot fulfill 4 and 5, be prepared to lead the rescuers back to your injured friend.

Everyone should acquire the basic knowledge of navigation. You use it every day, everywhere, just to get from one point to another. Once you learn the basics, you wonder why other people don't learn. It is so easy and so rewarding to be self-confident.

The tools used in navigation are your eyes, a compass, and a detailed map. The eyes you already use everyday. The map is simply a line picture

Map 175

that takes about ten minutes to understand. The compass is simply a needle that points one direction. You should understand the principle of any compass in about ten minutes. Using the three tools together takes about an hour of experimenting to get some acceptable results. Add a few hours of field practice to become proficient, and you have learned a skill that can help you every day of your life.

Man is one of the few mammals that has the ability to reason and analyze immediate and future problems. Map and compass are tools that help you to reason and analyze navigational problems accurately.

SIMPLE OUTDOOR NAVIGATION

All travel requires some type of navigation. In traveling from one point to another in the city or in the outdoors one uses visual landmarks, area maps, signs, or mental maps to find the route. Accurate return to your starting point will depend upon how well you remembered the landmarks you saw.

Simple Navigation — Used every day by everyone, everywhere.

Navigation is that knowledge of direction (visual, written, or mental) used when traveling from one place to another in a purposeful manner. It provides us with the knowledge of our exact location in relation to the point of origin or destination. We determine our position from landmarks, street signs, etc., that we see. Hence the eyes become a very important part of navigation. Without eyes to see and recognize these landmarks, we are lost. (A good example is fog or darkness.)

Landmarks — The visual checkpoints along your route.

City Landmarks		Rural Landmarks
House	All must be seen	Peak or hill
Store	and recognized	Cabin
School	to be of naviga-	Meadow
Railroad	tional value.	River
Street		Valley
Street Signs (North,		Trail
East, South, West)		Blaze on tree
Signal		Sun, stars, moon

Often we overlook the fact that landmarks are used every day by every person. These are checkpoints or reference points that guide us everywhere we go. In familiar surroundings, such as our homes, we know the position of every chair, table, door, bed, etc. Outdoors in unfamiliar territory, one must observe every turning point, creek crossing, slide area, peak, mountain range, etc.

The traveler must observe and remember these landmarks and be able to recognize them from all directions, going and returning. These landmarks then are the natural street signs of the outdoors. Failure to observe these, or to improvise check points when no natural features are prominent, can cause the outdoorsman to become disoriented, confused — or lost.

Value of Observation

The use of the roving eye is a great asset in land navigation. Rural landmarks are the corner street signs of the wilderness areas.

A good example of the value of observation is the freeway exit sign. Miss your turn-off sign and you will have to drive many extra miles.

If landmarks are not visible due to adverse weather (fog, snow, rain) or darkness, then other directional aids must be used (map, compass, radar, etc.).

Map   **177**

Maps

A map is a drawn or printed picture of the land as seen from above. Maps are available in many scales and sizes. The most common map in use by sportsmen is a planimetric map e.g., county or trail map) which shows only land features such as roads, trails, rivers, lakes and peak elevations. This map is best used from the city to the road end only (not nearly enough detail for wilderness travel).

For the sportsman who plans to travel off the trail — hunter, fisherman, hiker — a topographical contour map can be helpful. This map shows land shapes and elevations, with the shape of the land portrayed by lines following a picture of the ground surface at a constant elevation above sea level.

Many years ago map makers decided to draw all maps along latitude and longitude lines with all maps oriented to the same point on earth — the North Pole — with printed letters reading from west to east. North would be at the top of the map unless an illustrated compass or Map North arrow drawn on the map indicated otherwise.

Using a Map Properly

To use a street map one must first orient the map to the known street, placing the street map parallel to the known street, with Map North pointing to the North Pole.

Or — Put two positively identified visible landmarks not on the same line in alignment with their drawn map symbols.

Or — Correlate the ground landmarks and their map symbols by means of a compass.

Aids to General Direction Finding

Sun	East to west
Moon	East to west
Stars	North Star
Wind	Local prevailing wind
Contours	Valleys and ridges
Street signs	Trails signs, markers
Baseline	

A baseline is any unmistakable natural feature — a road, river, ridge, etc. — which runs along one entire boundary of your travel area, which you can see at all times and instantly know its direction and relationship to base camp and your present position.

A well known fact is that relatively few stream fishermen ever get lost. Why? Because they are beside their baseline at all times, and the flow of water always tells them the direction of camp.

Using the baseline for quick orientation is by far the simplest form of outdoor navigation, as long as visibility is good. Should weather obscure the baseline, the outdoorsman must refer to map and compass for orientation.

Many Maps to Choose From

Mental Map — Mental pictures of the area, from oral descriptions, visual pictorial maps, or previous experience.

Planimetric Maps — Flat maps that show streets, roads, trails, rivers towns and peak elevations.

Topographic Maps — Show all that planimetric maps do plus showing land shapes and elevations, portrayed by lines following the ground surface at a constant elevation above sea level.

Old Maps — Civil progress and nature often make maps obsolete. New roads, new trails, dams, cities arise. The cost of changing maps each year is uneconomical, so the responsibility of an up-to-date map rests with the user.

Hand Drawn Maps — These are the direction aids given by others and accuracy depends upon the maker.

All maps require a visual check of landmarks at turn points, or the absolute correct measurement of each leg and the exact angle of turn, in degrees, of the course being followed.

Value of Maps

You used a map, either a mental map or a drawn map, to get to your present location — this building, this room, the chair you are sitting in.

Map   179

Maps are directional aids that show, through drawn lines or mental checkpoints, the location of buildings, roads, rivers, and other natural features.

Interpretation of Topographic Maps

Symbols are the graphic language of maps — their shape, size, location, and color all have a special significance. The interpretation of contour maps is quite simple. The elevation lines tell the story. Widely spaced lines indicate a gentle slope; lines that run together, a cliff. A valley makes a patter of V's pointing upstream. A ridge appears as a downhill-pointing V or U, depending upon the sharpness of the ridge crest. Closed circles or loops indicate summits or depressions. By studying these contour lines before a planned trip, it is possible to get a mental picture of the shape of the land, its danger areas and checkpoints, and to choose the best time — and energy-saving route.

Altogether too many novice outdoorsmen do not carry adequate maps while traveling in unfamiliar territory. They assume trail signs and road signs will give them direction. Unfortunately, these signs and most landmarks may be obscured by poor visibility, deep snow, or destroyed by fire or vandals.

Marine charts and topographic maps mark the magnetic compass declination angle in degrees on each map. Many maps do not have any declination noted on the map, so it is important that you commit the degree angle of your locality to memory. In Washington State 22° East of North is the declination angle between magnetic north (where compass arrow points) and Map North (North Pole).

The only time declination must be used is in orienting the map to look like (line up with) the ground. All maps are drawn on latitude lines to the North Pole and must be oriented to these latitude lines each time the map is used. When using the compass for plotting directions to or from the map, or in straight line travel, magnetic or needle north bearings are sufficient.

Compass and Its Use

It is a well known fact that a compass, by itself, is inadequate as a direction finder or position locator unless the outdoorsman notes every compass bearing from the beginning of the trip. The greatest value of a compass is in orienting the map north to the North Pole when landmarks are obscured. Placing the map so that all landmarks on the map are in proper relationship to their land positions is of extreme importance to the outdoorsman attempting to find his position before plotting his direction home. A good example of man's inability to know his relative position to the North Pole at all times is to have everyone point to north with the eyes covered or in darkness.

Few compasses point to the North Pole. Most compasses point to what is commonly known as "needle north" or magnetic north, a geographic point somewhere near upper Greenland. The difference between the North Pole and north magnetic pole is called the angle of declination. The angle between these two points varies as one travels east or west, and the angle of declination, in degrees, will be noted on all good maps, to facilitate orienting the map properly.

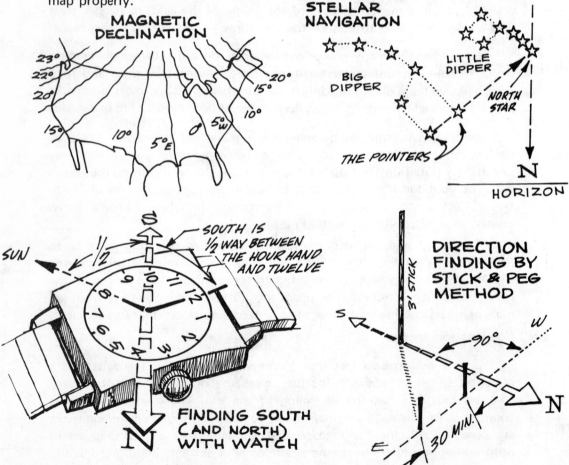

MAGNETIC DECLINATION

STELLAR NAVIGATION

BIG DIPPER

LITTLE DIPPER

NORTH STAR

THE POINTERS

N

HORIZON

SUN

SOUTH IS ½ WAY BETWEEN THE HOUR HAND AND TWELVE

FINDING SOUTH (AND NORTH) WITH WATCH

DIRECTION FINDING BY STICK & PEG METHOD

3' STICK

90°

30 MIN.

Orientation

In the field the map must be oriented to line up with the landmarks on the ground. This is accomplished by using the direction of landmarks on the ground and matching them, directionwise, with symbols on the map, or correlating the two by means of a compass.

To orient the map by using a compass, place the map on a flat surface, away from metal objects which could deflect the magnetic needle of the compass. Place the compass on the map so that the North-South line on the compass dial (the 360°-180° line) is parallel with the map north arrow or the vertical lines on the map. The map and compass are then turned carefully, as a unit, until the needle of the compass is separated from North (360°) by the proper declination indicated on the lower part of the topographical map.

Another good way to orient a map that has a magnetic north arrow noted on the map is to extend the Mag. North line across the map with a straight edge and pencil. To orient the map, place the compass base on or beside the extended line. Now rotate the map and compass slowly until the needle arrow is parallel to the extended line.

TOP OF MAP ALWAYS NORTH UNLESS OTHERWISE STATED

BORDER OF MAP AND MOST GRID LINES RUN NORTH-SOUTH, EAST-WEST

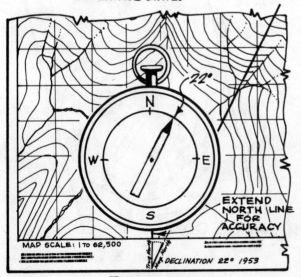

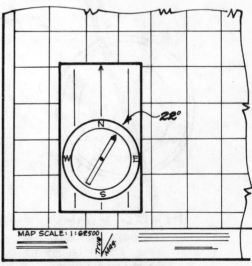

FIXED DIAL

MOVABLE DIAL

Using the Map to Find an Unknown Visible Landmark

With the map oriented and your position on the map known, it is possible to match up every visible landmark in the map area with its map symbol by putting the eye close to the map and sighting along a straight-edged marker from the known position to the visible landmark.

Finding Your Unknown Position with a Map

At times an outdoorsman does not know his point position, but is certain he is somewhere along a particular line — a ridge, trail or river. With a distant landmark, not on this line, positively identified, he can find his point position along the known line.

Using a compass, orient the map to Map North. Then determine the angle or magnetic bearing the positively identified landmark is away from the current position on the river, trail or ridge. This magnetic bearing line can be drawn onto the oriented map. Where the drawn line intersects the known position line is the sportsman's current point position.

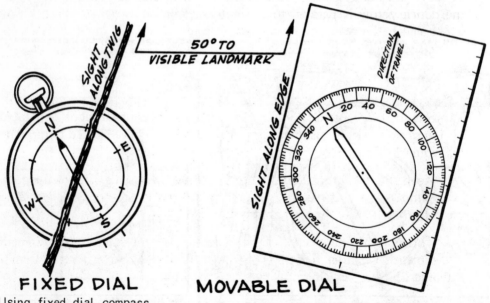

FIXED DIAL

Using fixed dial compass sight along a stick across the face and center of the compass.

MOVABLE DIAL

Using movable dial compass sight along the straight edge.

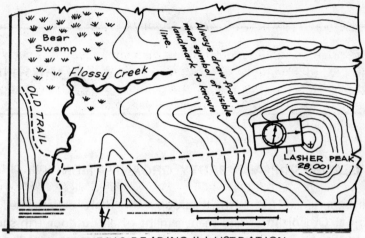

Within the illustration:
- Bear Swamp
- Flossy Creek
- OLD TRAIL
- *Always draw from map symbol of visible landmark to known line.*
- LASHER PEAK 28,001

MAGNETIC BEARING ILLUSTRATION

Magnetic bearings are determined by reading the angle in degrees
toward the landmark when the compass needle points to 360°
North (no declination needed)

Responsibility is Yours Alone

Once you embark upon a trip into the wilderness (where there are no
street signs), the map you carry — be it a mental map, a hand drawn map,
or the best topographic map you can buy, is the drawn picture of the land
around you. You alone have the responsibility of using it properly, checking
it often, and observing the landmarks you pass. Trusting others to do this
for you is foolhardy. Because of the rugged environment and the changeable
elements in the wilderness, you can suddenly find yourself alone, separated
by fog or storm or a mistaken turn, from those you have trusted to navigate
for you.

Keep the party together at all times. Under adverse conditions the combined knowledge and resources of all in the party will be needed to find
the way home.

Topographic maps may be purchased locally (see the Yellow Pages
under maps). Or order from U.S. Geological Survey, Denver Federal Center
Building 25, Denver, Colorado 80225.

U.S. Forest Service maps are available free in local Ranger Stations or
by mail from District offices through out the United States

II LEADERSHIP

LEADERSHIP AND PARTY ORGANIZATION

The less experienced an outdoor group, the more experienced the leader should be. Organization and management of an outdoor trip should be to minimize the work and increase the safety and enjoyment of the trip. Experienced leadership is a must for party safety in all wilderness or outdoor travel. The leader should plan the schedule and analyze in advance the area, terrain, weather and physical capabilities of those he plans to lead.

Organization of an Outdoor Party

Leader — Must be experienced, and must be aware of all facets of the type of activity planned, and have imagination and initiative to carry many responsibilities.

Assistant Leader — Competent to lead the group home should the leader be incapacitated. To help the leader discharge his many duties.

Who Can Go and who cannot go on a particular outing? This decision should rest with the leader, *who will be responsible for their conduct, safety, and well-being from the beginning to the end* of the outing.

Choosing the Party — The leader must look at each individual for these potential problems:

Mental attitude (soreheads, fearful, nonconformist).
Physical condition (weak, strong, medical problems).
Clothing and equipment
Experience — the less experienced, the more guidance needed.
Analyze each person for woodsmanship, equipment use.

Leader's Group Equipment

Any party planning one or more days away from civilization should carry all their probable needs:

> Group First Aid Kit (refer to Appendix)
> A sleeping bag is handy for treatment of shock in the event of an injury.
> Group special equipment (refer to Appendix)
> Group shelter (refer to Appendix)

A leader's responsibilities are many. He must find the best route, check everyone's equipment, administer first aid, supervise camp, and provide for safe transportation. He must plan the trip schedule and give instructions in a firm but cheerful voice. The following list includes only a few of the responsibilities of a competent leader.

Before Leaving Town

Choose an assistant leader and other help.

Be informed of, or familiar with the travel area.

Procure up-to-date maps of the area.

Set a minimum and maximum number of people wanted on the trip.

Inquire into the physical capabilities and limitations of every member.

Provide a required list of personal equipment to each member and check his gear before leaving.

Inform at least one responsible person of the exact trip location, transportation used, trip schedule, estimated time of return, number in the party, equipment carried, experience of the leader, and emergency plans. (Someone in town and available).

Acquire fire permits, camping permits, or any special permits to trespass on private or government property.

Acquire necessary minor releases and obtain insurance required by your organization.

Plan and map several safe routes for avoiding potential hazard areas (avalanche, rockfall, etc.).

Carry only first class equipment, whether it be new or used.

Plan transportation to and from the area.

Plan for delays. Arrange for responsible people to advise companies, bosses, schools and parents in the event of unavoidable delay. Arrange for someone to feed the dog and milk the cow, and eliminate the necessity of having to meet a deadline.

Before Leaving the Car

Pinpoint your location on the map. Make notes of landmarks and establish a base line to help your return trip. Do this with several members of the party.

Check with local authority as to trail changes or area restrictions.

Sign out with local authorities (Ranger, Forest Service). Leave a schedule in the car window if no authority is near.

Remind the party of trail rules (smoking, use of alcohol, littering, trail etiquette) and rescue procedures.

Park cars clear of roads and trails and be sure they can get out in case of emergency. Do not block the way for snow removal equipment.

Leaders' Responsibilities on the Trail

Appoint a person to be rear guard.

Keep the party together and have a head count often. Be alert for the wanderer.

Call short rest stops for equipment adjustment, water and energy intake, and nature calls.

While stopped, verify your position on the map.

Choose the best route for the party. Never take the group beyond the capabilities of the individuals — mental or physical. Problem areas may require a change of route.

Be alert for physical condition changes of individuals, such as fatigue, injuries, sunburn, blisters, etc. Here you must be both doctor and psychologist.

Watch the weather. If it turns bad, camp; turn back; get to shelter. With lightning get off the ridges.

Teach as you travel (map, compass, woodsmanship, conservation, survival).

Instill confidence in the party members by doing the right things and making good decisions (not always alone).

Leaders' Responsibilities at Camp

Camp organization
Latrines
Pure water
Safe fire
Safe food protection (sun, animals, weather)
Enforce proper use of axes, guns, saws, boats
Safe shelters (watch for flash flood, avalanche or rockfall areas, dead
     snags, fire, lightning, wind, rain).
Good outdoor ethics (moral obligation to the young to set a good
     example)
Keep the party together (no evening hiking alone).
Always use proper hiking techniques, good judgment in decisions,
     proper language in instructing the young.
Teach others about safe outdoor travel and the wonders of nature that
     abound around them during their journey.

Leaders' Responsibilities Back at the Car

Tally members of the party; are you still all together?

Stowage of *all* equipment used.

Sign back in with proper authorities that you have returned; give them reports on trail conditions, camp conditions, and potential dangers noticed.

Leaders' Responsibilities to the Organization

Report to parents any injuries, equipment loss, merits (or demerits?) of young members of the party.

Report to the organization's authorities on the completion of the trip, problems encountered, recommendations for future trips, number of persons in the party, and conduct.

In addition to all of the above, the leader may wish to tutor one of the party to be the leader of the next outing.

Responsibilities of Individual Members of the Hiking Party

When a person joins a group, he relinquishes his individual preferences for the good of the party.

Many hikers have been subjected to unpleasant experiences by using poor or ill-fitting equipment. Worse yet, many a trip has been spoiled for a whole group or even cancelled because of one person's failure to provide himself with adequate gear.

To safely enjoy the outdoors, one must start with good boots that fit properly and warm clothing that serves all his needs.

Recommended Group Equipment (Leader's Responsibility)

Large cook pots

Gasoline stove — lantern — fuel

Large metal storage cans (to protect supplies from animals)

Ropes, pitons, carabiners, rescue gear.

Water containers — and purification supplies.

Signal equipment.

Recommended Group Shelter (Leader's responsibility)

Tents and extra guy ropes
Ground cloths

Shovel, saw, axe
Plus any seasonal equipment.

Recommended Group First Aid Supplement Kit (Leader's responsibility)

2   Triangle bandages
2   Ace bandages
4   Large compress
    Snake bite kit
    Burn ointment
    Eye wash

Green soap
Scissors
Tweezers
Air splint
2" adhesive tape

Plus all essentials of the individual First Aid kit.

Individual Personal Equipment:

Clothing — warm, layers, loose fitting (wool preferred), with rain clothes.
Boots — well fitting (lug soles for firm footing preferred)
Extra socks — wool for warmth and cushioning
Eye protection — reflected or direct sun
Head protection — Body heat loss, sunburn, mosquitos.

Small Pack to carry the trail essentials
Extra clothes — complete change
Extra Food — emergency (2 meals)
First aid kit (see Appendix II)
Knife   )
Candle   ) Fire
Matches, waterproofed) Starting
Flashlight   )
Map, up-to-date) Direction
Compass   )
Plastic tarp — tent
Water canteen

Extras
Female problems
Special medicine
Extra prescription
   eyeglasses
30' shroud line
Insect repellent
Toilet paper
High energy nibble foods
Soap and towel
Toothbrush

Plus special equipment needed for specific environment or activity, such as hunting, skiing, boating, camping special equipment.

RECOMMENDED FIRST AID KIT

ITEM	AMOUNT	USE and COMMENT
Tape, not waterproof	2" roll on cardboard	Flattened, will take less space
Triangular Bandage	One	Cut on bias from 40" cloth
Band-aids	4 to 6, 3/4" or 1"	For small lacerations
Steri-pads (gauze flats)	4, 3" x 3"	For larger wounds
Vaseline Gauze Pads	2, 3" x 3"	For burns or abrasions
Burn ointment	1 tube, 1/3 or 1/2 oz.	For sunburn (Foile, Amertan, etc.)
Holocaine HC1 eye ointment	1 tube, 1/6 oz.	For pain from snowblindness; small amount under eyelids every four hours
Amoply Ammonia Inhalants	3 tubes	For hornet, bee, and other insects' bites
Needle	1 medium size	
Razor blade	1 single edge	For shaving hairy spots before taping
Aspirin	1/2 to 1 dozen tablets	For pain; one to two every four hours
Salt tablets (enteric coated)	1 to 2 dozen tablets	One whenever cramps occur or when perspiring heavily. Drinking water essential.
Antacid	1/2 dozen tablets	For nausea; may be Amphogel, Gelusil, Tums, etc.
Antihistamine	1/2 dozen tablets	For insect bites, colds, or hives; one tablet every four hours
Gauze roll	1, 2" roll	
Safety pins	6 each	
Scissors	Small pair	
Old pair of individual's prescription glasses, if needed for travel vision.		

Following items need a doctor's prescription:

ITEM	AMOUNT	USE and COMMENT
Darvon	1/2 dozen tablets	For severe pain; 2 tablets every 4 hours
Dexedrine Sulfate 5mgm.	2 to 4 tablets	Severe exhaustion; 1 every 4 hours for two doses, then 1 every 6 hours. Sleep essential.

Overnight emergency provisions you can fabricate in a few minutes at home from kitchen and garage supplies.

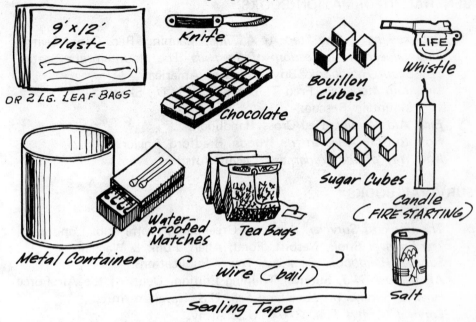

PERSONAL SURVIVAL KIT

A suitable container may be found in a pint turpentine or thinner can which has been thoroughly cleaned and dried. Cut the top off and remove sharp burrs.

Put all small items in plastic sandwich bags to keep them dry. Add bandaids, medication, spare prescription lens, needle and thread, safety pins, and other small vital necessities.

In just a few minutes you can assemble and package the components of this kit so that you may be prepared for a short-term emergency situation. To reseal the can, fashion a lid from plastic and tape securely in place.

Such a kit, homemade or purchased, cannot help you survive a storm unless it is available when needed. Always carry it whenever you travel away from civilization.

RECOMMENDED BOOKS AND FILMS

GENERAL INFORMATION BOOKS

Backpacking — One Step At A Time, Manning, Rec. Coop. Seattle.
Mountaineering — Freedom of the Hills, The Mountaineers, Seattle.
Boy Scout Handbook. Boy Scouts of America.
Mountain Medicine. Fred T. Darvill, Jr., M.D., Skagit
    Mountain Rescue.
First Aid Manual. Red Cross Handbook.
How to Stay Alive in the Woods. Bradford Angier.
New Way of the Wilderness. Calvin Rutstrum.

SURVIVAL BOOKS

The Book of Survival, Anthony Greenbank, Wolfe Pub. London.
The Survival Book, Nesbitt, Pond, Allen, Funk & Wagnalls
Survival Handbook. Cassiday. Tower Publications.
AF Manual 64-3, Survival Training Edition. Dept. of the Air Force.
How to Survive on Land and Sea. U.S. Naval Institute.
Survival (Army) F.M. 21-76. U.S. Army.
Food in the Wilderness. G.W. Martin and R.W. Scott.
Primitive Medical Aid. Life Support Technology.
Poisonous Plants of the Wilderness. Life Support Technology.
Surviving the Unexpected Curriculum Guide, Survival Ed. Assn.

FILMS

The Thermal Wilderness (Effect of heat). SAFECO Insurance Co.
By Nature's Rules (Effect of cold). SAFECO Insurance Co.
Lost Hunter (Psychological effect). Film Original, Boise, Idaho.
Survival Stress (Psychological effect). A.F. — TF 1-5375. Air Force.
Survival — Mountain & Desert (General). A.F. — TF-5571A.
    Air Force.
Mountains Don't Care (Mountain). Mountain Rescue Association.
Castles in the Snow (Winter). Life Support Technology.
Snow How (Winter — mechanical). Life Support Technology.
Out of the Sea (Beach). Life Support Technology.
Edible Plants of Field and Forest. Local film libraries.
Survival Films and Slides. National Rifle Association.

INDEX

Other survival films are available from:

    Visual Education and Audio-Visual Centers of State Universities.
    Military Film Libraries
    Civil Defense Coordinators — Local, State, and Federal
      Civil Defense also has many brochures regarding the subject.

Survival Course Curriculum Guide for this book.

    Surviving the Unexpected   75 Pages by Dan & Gene Fear
                        Paper 8½ x 11 Comb $2.50
      Covers Wilderness Survival and Survival from
    Natural and Man-Made Disasters — Classroom and Field Problems.